GOD IN FLESH MADE MANIFEST

Sermons For Advent,
Christmas And Epiphany
Cycle A, Gospel Lesson Texts

MARK WM. RADECKE

CSS Publishing Company, Inc.
Lima, Ohio

GOD IN FLESH MADE MANIFEST

Library of Congress Cataloging-In-Publication Data

Radecke, Mark William.
  God in flesh made manifest : sermons for Advent, Christmas, and Epiphany, : Cycle A, gospel lesson texts / Mark Wm. Radecke.
      p. cm.
   ISBN 0-7880-0485-9
   1. Advent sermons. 2. Christmas sermons. 3. Epiphany season — Sermons. 4. Bible. N. T. Gospels — Sermons. 5. Serrmons, American. I. Title.
BV4254.5.R33   1995
252'.61—dc20   95-13428
                                                                                                      CIP

This book is available in the following formats, listed by ISBN:
0-7880-0485-9 Book
0-7880-0486-7 IBM 3 1/2 computer disk
0-7880-0487-5 IBM 3 1/2 book and disk package
0-7880-0488-3 Macintosh computer disk
0-7880-0489-1 Macintosh book and disk package
0-7880-0490-5 IBM 5 1/4 computer disk
0-7880-0491-3 IBM 5 1/4 book and disk package

PRINTED IN U.S.A.

Acknowledgements

Appreciation is expressed to HarperCollins Publishers, Inc., for permission to quote material from *Pilgrim At Tinker Creek*, copyright 1974 by Annie Dillard.

I express my personal thanks and gratitude to:

Linda Akers for her able secretarial assistance;

the people of Christ Lutheran Church, Roanoke, Virginia, who figure prominently in and behind many of these sermons (some of which they will doubtless recognize); and

to my wife Tami whose advent in my life has been and is an epiphany, for her constant encouragement, interest and support.

for Tami
on
our wedding day

October 8, 1994

Editor's Note Regarding The Lectionary

During the past two decades there has been an attempt to move in the direction of a uniform lectionary among various Protestant denominations.

•Lectionary Uniformity

Preaching on the same scripture lessons every Sunday is a step in the right direction of uniting Christians of many faiths. If we are reading the same scriptures together we may also begin to accomplish other achievements. Our efforts will be strengthened through our unity.

•Christian Unity

Beginning with Advent 1995 The Evangelical Lutheran Church in America will drop its own lectionary schedule and adopt the Revised Common Lectionary.

•ELCA Adopts Revised Common Lectionary

We at CSS Publishing Company heartily embrace this change. We recognize, however, that there will be a transitional period during which some churches may continue for a time to use the traditional Lutheran lectionary. In order to accommodate these clergy and churches who may still be referring to the Lutheran lectionary we will for a period of time continue to provide sermons and illustrations based on scriptural passages from BOTH the Lutheran and The Revised Common lectionaries.

•For Those In Transition

Table Of Contents

C — Revised Common Lectionary; L — Lutheran Lectionary; RC — Roman Catholic Lectionary

Advent 1
Matthew 24:36-44 (C)
Matthew 24:37-44 (L, RC)

Come, Lord Jesus, Quickly Come!

The same thing has, I'm sure, happened to you: you live your whole life without seeing or hearing a certain word or phrase or expression, and then you see or hear it two or three times within a relatively short period.

The first time I saw this particular phrase was a few years back at a synod assembly. I attended a small group session led by a pastor who had just returned from Nicaragua and El Salvador. He was showing some of his slides to help us understand the political and economic situation in those troubled lands.

About midway through his presentation, one of the slides showed what I took at first to be an outdoor chapel or worship area. There were pews and kneelers, and up front, an altar. Grass and weeds, about a foot high, were growing in the aisle and under and around the pews as well. But then I saw that this was — or had been — a building. At least one of the walls was visible in the slide.

The pastor explained that this was indeed a Roman Catholic church which had been bombed out in the recent violence. The roof had caved in and the walls had gaping holes blown out of them. The incoming rain and sun had allowed the grass and weeds to grow among the rubble.

The next slide showed a close-up of some graffiti that had been spray-painted on a wall, beneath a depiction of Christ on the cross.

In other slides, we had seen many political and revolutionary slogans similarly spray-painted on walls. But this one was different. I neither read nor speak Spanish. I didn't need it in order to recognize the oldest and most passionate prayer of Christianity: "Pronto viene, Jesus Christo." Come quickly, Jesus Christ.

Into this world of mindless murder, bloodshed and bombing — come quickly.

Into this insane world where men and women disappear under cover of night and are never heard from again, where children are gunned down in the streets and in their own homes — quickly come.

A prayer, a cry of profound anguish and suffering and yet also of profound hope born of faith, spray-painted in flat black, beneath a crucified Christ, bidding him to come, and come *pronto*.

Several weeks after that assembly on my way to Danbury, Connecticut, for the ordination of a friend, I passed by an area across the river from New York's Spanish Harlem. One of the fields along the highway was a dumping ground for about two dozen stolen or abandoned cars and trucks. Most were burned out, completely stripped, completely rusted. One was parked close to the shoulder of the highway. A four-door sedan it was — or had been. The dull orange of the rust and the black soot from the smoke provided the background for a bright red bumper sticker someone had pasted on the car's trunk. It read: "Pronto viene, Jesus Christo."

In North America's urban blight and decay no less than in Central America's violence and revolution, the same cry, the same prayer, "Come quickly, Jesus Christ!"

So the promise of Jesus as recorded in Matthew is: "The Son of Man is coming at an unexpected hour." It is a restatement of Malachi's prophecy: "The Lord whom you seek will suddenly come to his temple. Behold he is coming, says the Lord of hosts."

And so we say in our eucharistic prayer, "Amen, come, Lord Jesus." And in our Advent prayers: "Stir up, O Lord, your power and come."

The last words of the New Testament, "Maranatha. Amen, come, Lord Jesus," echo and answer the last words of the prophet Isaiah: "Oh, that thou wouldst rend the heavens and come down."

Come down, come quickly, come *pronto*. Suddenly come into this house of doom, this chamber of corruption and despair. Break down its walls and set us free. Come. And come quickly.

Jesus describes his return as an event, not a process. As sudden as the flood that inundated the globe in the Noah story, so sudden will be the coming of the Son of Man. Those who eagerly await this coming are called to be awake, alert, ready, for no warning will be given: the Son of Man will come suddenly and at an hour known only to his Father.

But how long can even the most ardent believer sustain such "red alert" readiness? A week? An Advent season? Surely not a lifetime! The prior question is: What constitutes readiness? The old Adam and old Eve think instinctively in terms of moral readiness: Live in such a way that the sudden return will find our behavioral slates clean. We have, however, lived too long and accumulated too many experiences of our moral frailty to believe we can ever be morally ready for one whose standard is perfection.

This Advent, I invite you to think instead in terms of spiritual readiness: Live in such a way that the cry, "Pronto viene, Jesus Christo," is a natural expression of your heart's true desire for the Lord's sudden and promised return. The old Adam and old Eve fear such a return, for they know it spells their doom.

But like those unprepared in the Noah story, the old Adam and Eve have been drowned — in this case, drowned in the waters of baptism. From those waters, a new being in Christ arises: one whose heart cries out, "Come, Lord Jesus. Quickly come."

Come quickly to the brutal terror of oppressive regimes, to the grinding poverty of center cities, to the mindless cruelty that paints swastikas on synagogues, to the fear and emptiness of our own lives: come quickly.

And until you come, we will — by your grace — trust and wait and pray, and work and live by the values of your coming kingdom.

Living by those values sometimes sets us in opposition to the ways of the present age and present neo-pagan culture with its values and assumptions. So our text speaks honestly of "two in the field; one will be taken and one left. Two grinding meal; one taken, one left."

Until that day, we give thanks to our Lord and bless his name for allowing us to glimpse his coming: in the miracle of human reconciliation; in the too-rare efforts of nations to talk out rather than shoot out their differences; in the opportunity to serve our Lord by serving his poor and needy ones all around us; in the bread and wine of the eucharist, in which God comes to us, and by which he makes of us a community, a forgiven family of his children.

In all these things and countless others, he comes to us. Not yet fully, but enough to make our hearts long for and yearn for and ache for that day when he does; and in the meanwhile, to be about the peacemaking, reconciling, life-affirming work God has entrusted to us.

And so we pray, "Stir up our hearts, O Lord, to prepare the way for your only Son. By his coming, give us strength in our conflicts and shed light on our path through the darkness of this world."

Create in us new hearts, O God. And renew a right spirit within us. Hearts and spirits that reach out, and join in the ardent prayer of our brothers and sisters of every time and every place: "Pronto viene, Jesus Christo." Maranatha! Come, Lord Jesus, quickly come.

The Baptist's Prophecy

In her Pulitzer Prize winning book, *Pilgrim at Tinker Creek*, author Annie Dillard recalls this chilling remembrance:

"I see tonight the picture of a friendly member of the forest service in Wisconsin, who is freeing a duck frozen onto the ice, by chopping out its feet with a hand axe. It calls to mind the spare, cruel story Thomas McGonigle told me about herring gulls frozen on ice off Long Island. When his father was young, he used to walk out on Great South Bay, which had frozen over, and frozen the gulls to it. Some of the gulls were already dead. He would take a hunk of driftwood and brain the living gulls; then, with a steel knife, he hacked them free below the body and rammed them into a burlap sack. The family ate herring gull all winter, close around a lighted table in a steamy room. And out on the bay, the ice was studded with paired red stumps." [1]

It is not an uncommon occurrence. Water fowl descend upon frozen lakes and bays in winter. The warmth of their feet and bodies melts the ice which then refreezes, trapping them helplessly in an icy grip from which there is no escape except death or outside deliverance. It is not a pretty thought — but it is real. And it is equally real that some hungry opportunist should bash and hack the birds instead of attempting to set them free from their life-or-death predicament.

Today is the Second Sunday in Advent and we encounter in our gospel lesson John the Baptist, prophet and precursor of the promised Messiah, mysterious man of Advent.

What are we to make of a man who suddenly simply "appears" in the wilderness clothed in camel's hair with an animal pelt for a belt, eating locusts and wild honey?

Very little is actually known about this enigmatic figure. And consequently, many opinions are offered. But one thing at least is certain: In his vision of the coming one, he saw a mighty judge, an awesome and exacting king, someone of uncompromising righteousness who would no more hesitate to consign a sinner to the unquenchable fire with senses undiminished than you or I would hesitate to squash a cockroach.

In terms of the *Tinker Creek* image, John saw a figure walking across the ice, club in hand, ready to brain and bash every frozen soul and hack them from the ice with a steel knife, leaving a lake studded with paired red stumps.

As for the day that such a one would usher in, recall John's inaugural sermon: "You brood of vipers — who warned you to flee from the wrath to come? The axe is laid to the root of the trees; every tree which fails to bring forth good fruit is hewn down and cast into the fire. He is coming with his winnowing fork in his hand to clear the threshing floor and the chaff he will burn with unquenchable fire."

Matthew and Luke tell the story quite similarly, and in both cases John comes off like a wild man, a desert wanderer, a religious fanatic, an "end-of-the-world-is-near" prophet — judgmental and impatient. Indeed, this is usually how he is portrayed in movies and dramatizations.

The Baptist in Mark and John's Gospels is decidedly more restrained, but still with an unqualified emphasis on repentance and sinfulness, on the approaching day of judgment, on the power of the coming one who will baptize with the Holy Spirit and with fire and storm.

Again, to use the *Tinker Creek* image, you who hear the prophet are a helpless herring gull, frozen fast to the ice. And for all your flapping, flailing, and crying you are unable to free yourself. The coming one of the Baptist's prophecy is the Righteous and Almighty, crossing the ice with driftwood club and steel knife in hand. When he comes to you he will stop. He will examine you and judge you.

If you are found wanting — *and you will be!* — he will bash your brains out with the club, hack you from the ice, ram you into a burlap sack and leave behind a lake studded with a pair of red stumps. In short, my friends, we stand not a chance.

The Baptist's prophecy was a prophecy of the coming Judge, and his dreaded day of wrath. Doesn't it seem at least a little strange to you, then, that Mark should choose to begin his Gospel with the proclamation of this prophet, and even introduce it with the words: "The beginning of the *Good News* of Jesus Christ, the Son of God"? It does indeed seem strange, until we recall one crucial fact: the Gospel was not written until after the events of Good Friday and Easter Sunday.

Mark wants to show that the Baptist was the last of the great prophets, in line with those who untiringly called God's people back to the Lord, threatening them and warning them of the consequences of their actions.

When we attempt to know God apart from the divine self-revelation in Jesus Christ, we, too, encounter only a wrathful God displeased with our innumerable violations of his will and his law; a stern God sorely disappointed in the failure of his creatures; a judging God approaching us with driftwood club and steel knife poised and at the ready.

But when we take in the entire perspective of incarnation, crucifixion, and resurrection, we see that John's prophecy is indeed the beginning of the good news of Jesus Christ. And it is only the beginning.

It is the beginning because it points up sharply that human sinfulness is a radical problem which cannot go unchecked, and from which mere mortals cannot extricate themselves.

It is the beginning of the gospel because it points up that God has decided to come among us not simply because he thought it might be nice to do so, but because nothing short of his coming could turn this mess around.

It is the beginning of the gospel because it points up the fact that implicit in the very incarnation of God in Christ is a judgment and condemnation of human injustice and unrighteousness.

The Baptist's prophecy is the beginning of the gospel, but it is **only** the beginning of the gospel. By evangelical insight, it is the preaching of the law, the wrath of God, which necessarily precedes the preaching of the gospel which is the end of the law.

There are two things you can do when a herring gull is frozen to the ice: You can bash its brains out and hack it from the ice. Or you can chop the ice around its feet and thereby set it free.

From the perspective of John the Baptist, we would have no way of knowing which course God would choose with regard to us, frozen in our sin.

But from the perspective of the cross and empty tomb, we see that God chooses to free us from our helpless predicament at great cost and not to brain us because we got ourselves into the predicament in the first place.

The Baptist's prophecy is truly the beginning of the good news of Jesus Christ, the Son of God. It serves as a constant reminder of what God could have done *to us*. But thank God it is only the beginning. The rest of the gospel tells us what God has indeed done *for us*.

An Advent hymn concludes with these words: "He comes to judge the nations, a terror to his foes, a light of consolation and blessed hope to those who love the Lord's appearing. O glorious Sun, now come; send forth your beams so cheering and guide us safely home."

Like newly released herring gulls, we thank our liberator for using the two-edged sword of his word on the ice and not on us. We appreciate our freedom to fly and soar like we've never appreciated it before. May we vow never to freeze ourselves solid by standing too long in one place again.

---

1. Annie Dillard, *Pilgrim At Tinker Creek*, Bantam Books, 1974, pp. 42-43.

Would We Rather Be Comfortable Or Comforted?

"What did you go out into the wilderness to look at?" Jesus asks the crowd. "Someone dressed in soft robes? Those who wear soft robes are in royal palaces. What then did you go out to see? A prophet? Yes, I tell you, and more than a prophet." The crowds went out to see one arrayed not in comfortable soft raiment but in the rugged prophet's garb of camel hair and leather.

The old saw has it that the preacher's task is to comfort the afflicted... and afflict the comfortable.

As we approach our Advent scriptures this morning, it occurs to me: There is a world of difference between being comfort*ed* and being comfort*able*, a difference as stark as the difference between soft raiment and camel's hair.

Being comfortable implies, at least in our culture, an absence of disturbing, distressing features in one's life. More specifically, it carries the connotation of a standard of living that is more than sufficient. And so we say: "She makes a comfortable salary. They enjoy a very comfortable lifestyle."

When we look for synonyms, we think of such words as *content*, *untroubled*, *carefree* and *secure*. All of these things, taken together, give the term *comfortable* the faint aroma of complacency and a whiff of self-satisfaction.

Some who are comfortable protect their comfortableness by choosing to avoid the disturbing, distressing and painful features of this life and these times. Hunger, homelessness, and violence; fires in California, earthquakes in India, floods in the American heartland; genuine give-and-take, listen-as-well-as-speak debates over the morality of abortion, homosexuality and gun control; to say nothing about the quiet desperation of many individuals, the substitution of family busyness for family cohesiveness, the collapse of community and the resulting loneliness that is the identifying characteristic of life in late twentieth century suburban America: all of these things and dozens more are guaranteed to make us *un*comfortable. Those who are determined to keep their comfort level high therefore avoid dealing with these things, or at least minimize their exposure to them.

Let's be careful: Not all people of wealth are comfortable in this sense of the word, nor does one have to be wealthy to be comfortable in this way. What one needs to be in order to be comfortable in this way is apathetic, dispassionate, detached, aloof and/or very, very good at denial. The sad truth is: Too many of us *are* comfortable, or wish we were, or strive to be. God does not join us or help us in our efforts to be comfortable. That's the bad news this Advent morning.

Here's the good news: God does comfort us. And we are comforted. To comfort means to soothe in distress or sorrow; to ease misery or grief; to bring consolation or hope. That is exactly what God did for Israel, speaking through the prophet Isaiah, when Israel was carried off from her beloved and comfortable homeland into exile in Babylon. Isaiah announces that Israel's oppression in a foreign land has come to an end, that God is about to lead his people on a second exodus. That promise, from the God who rules history and moves events to accomplish his purpose, brings comfort to God's people in their distress, sorrow, misery and grief. They are consoled and given hope. They are, in a word, comforted.

But they are *not* made comfortable: Hard work awaits the returned exiles. Their homeland lay in ruins; their temple destroyed; their economy collapsed. To discomforted people such as these, God can bring comfort. To those who are already comfortable, who are snug and smug in their self-sufficiency and security, the proclamation of God's comfort is meaningless.

So also, in Matthew's Gospel, John is in prison and has his disciples ask Jesus if Jesus is the Messiah. Jesus responds with the great good news that the blind see, the lame walk, lepers are cleansed, the deaf hear, the dead are raised and the poor have good news brought to them. In a word, the afflicted are comforted. But they are not made comfortable: John is a prophet, no reed shaken by the wind, no palace courtier nattily attired. He speaks words of great challenge as he introduces the coming of God's kingdom.

The old saw, that the preacher's task is to comfort the afflicted and afflict the comfortable, proclaims a profound theological truth. For when we are afflicted, that is when God comforts us. If we are comfortable, God must first penetrate our false security. Only then can the news of the Messiah's coming strike our ears as a word of comfort.

So what of us this Advent? Would we rather be comfort*ed* or comfort*able*? Would we prefer to be apathetic, dispassionate, detached, and aloof; unsullied by the woes and weariness of the world, and of our own lives; unmoved and untouched by the very things God's promised and the coming Messiah came to remedy?

Or are we spiritually prepared to immerse ourselves in the rugged world to which the Savior came, trusting God's promise to comfort us when the load becomes heavy, the grief intense, the sorrow and misery unbearable? For some of us, that might mean going to ghettoes and barrios, nursing homes, prisons or mental institutions. For others, it means sharing the grief, sorrow or misery of a neighbor, a fellow member of the church, a co-worker. It means being for that person a conduit of God's comfort, an incarnation of God's comforting presence, a messenger who gently and unapologetically shares how the birth of the Babe of Bethlehem and his subsequent life, death and resurrection comforts him or her, and by this sharing offers consolation and hope that are more rugged and durable than soft raiments and reeds shaken by the wind.

Before we can speak that word, we need to hear it. Listen, people of God: people who want to know and love God, people who want to know and love one another, but who are afraid.

Afraid of giving up control, yet burdened by the perceived demand to stay on top of everything.

Afraid of inadequacy, yet wanting to help.

Afraid of giving away too much — of money or of self — yet wanting to be good stewards.

Afraid of mediocrity in ministry, yet reluctant to make the commitments of time, talent and treasure that make excellence achievable.

To you — precisely to you — in this your affliction, God comes to you. The signs of his coming are hidden, as they were hidden to the people in the time of Isaiah, Jesus and John. But now as well as then God's promise is trustworthy and true! That promise and that presence simply is your hope, rugged and durable. That promise and that presence come to you today, hidden again, under the forms of bread and wine.

The advent of the messiah, the promise and the presence — means by which God makes us not comfortable, but comforted. And thus comforted, we are truly equipped to "Go in peace and serve the Lord."

Advent 4
Matthew 1:18-25 (C, L)
Matthew 1:18-24 (RC)

Emmanuel: An Advent Dayenu

In the Jewish tradition there is a liturgy and accompanying song called "Dayenu." *Dayenu* is a Hebrew word which can be translated several ways. It can mean: "It would have been enough," or "we would have been grateful and content," or "our need would have been satisfied."

Part of the Dayenu is a responsive reading that goes like this:

> *O God, if thy only act of kindness was to deliver us from the bondage of Egypt, Dayenu! — It would have been enough.*
>
> *If thy only act of deliverance was to divide the Red Sea waters, Dayenu! — It would have been enough.*
>
> *If thy only act of mercy was to provide manna in the wilderness, Dayenu! — It would have been enough.*
>
> *If thy only act of graciousness was the gift of the sabbath day, Dayenu! — It would have been enough.*
>
> *If thy only act of love was to favor us with thy Torah, Dayenu! — It would have been enough.*
>
> *If thy only act of lovingkindness was to bring us into the land of Israel, Dayenu! — It would have been enough.*

The reading then concludes: "How grateful are we and how doubly blessed for all these acts of kindness and mercy and graciousness which the Lord our God has bestowed upon us."

Dayenu celebrates the multilayered grace and extravagant love of God.

The scriptures appointed for the Fourth Sunday in Advent remind me of the Dayenu. I believe it can help us as we seek to hear God's word to us through these texts today.

Both texts tell of the birth of a special child. "Behold," Isaiah prophesies, "a young woman shall conceive and bear a son and shall call his name Immanuel."

Matthew quotes that text in his Gospel and adds the explanation that Emmanuel means "God with us" or, more accurately, "God is with us."

In the movie *My Blue Heaven*, one character attempts to explain a situation to another. The second character, played by Steve Martin, keeps saying, "I'm wit-choo, I'm wit-choo." And then explains, "When I say I'm wit-choo, I don't mean it like an expression. I mean I'm wit-choo; I'*m* wit - *choo*!

Just so, the name of the promised baby Emmanuel, God with us, is far more than an expression. It means far more than that God understands us. It means that God is with us. Physically, truly with us. Not apart from us. Not up in heaven or off in some other world detached from and indifferent to our lives, our hopes and fears, our choices, decisions and indecisions, our thoughts and words and deeds; no: God is *with* us.

Jesus said it this way: "Wherever two or three are gathered together in my name, there am I" — where? — *in the midst of them*. And if we press the question, "Where in the midst of us?" the gospel gives these answers:

> In the bread and wine which are not only signs of his presence, but his body broken for us, his blood shed for us.

> In his word, in which he assures us of God's favor and love for us apart from any consideration of our naughtiness or niceness.

In the ministry of one believer to another, not only speaking words of comfort, but himself or herself embodying comfort, bringing Christ to another in his or her own ministry of caring and compassion.

In all these things, we know God as Emmanuel, God with us. If you are here this morning because you are seeking God, you have come to the right place. For here the wine is poured and here the bread is broken. Here the word is heard, for here the word is spoken. Here God's people seek to embody Christ in their love for one another, haltingly, at times, to be sure, and not without failure. But God was willing to take that risk by coming into our midst as a baby, and like a baby, we often stumble and fall. If God could take that risk, can we not respond in openness and trust?

Had God simply given us that much — a promise signifying that God is with us — Dayenu! That would have been enough. We would have been grateful and content. But there is more.

In Isaiah's day, the Assyrian empire had become the dominant power in the Middle East. It was threatening Judah and Judah's near neighbors. Calamity is about to befall the people of God. The heat is on. The pressure intense. We are besieged. "Where, now, is our God?" the people cry. Comes the answer: Emmanuel. God is with us.

This child is an embodied way for God to say what God and the angels so often say in scripture: "Fear not. I am with thee." "Fear not, for behold, I bring you good news of a great joy. For to you is born... a savior, Christ the Lord." And because this is so, we in faith can say with the psalmist, "Yea, though I walk through the valley of the shadow of death, I will fear no evil." Why? "For thou art *with me*."

When such fearsome foes as cancer and AIDS and debilitating disease and relentless pain assault us; when alcohol or chemical dependency, physical abuse or mental confusion, marital breakdown, or parent-child strife, dead-end job, or the news that "your department has been transferred; your position may be eliminated" comes in flat tones, shaking our foundations, that is when we cling with all our being to the hope-renewing sign of Emmanuel — an incarnate assurance that God is with us.

This baby, you see, is for us a way to keep the faith. For just when we are most tempted to believe that God has abandoned us or forgotten us or doesn't care a whit about our fate, God gives us a sign: Emmanuel, an embodied reminder that God is with us. Not merely that God understands, but that God is with us, beside us, among us, in our midst, to allay our fears, to save and comfort and console, and not to damn.

Had God simply given us *that* much — a child, an incarnation of the divine promise — Dayenu! That would have been enough. We would have been grateful and content. But there is more.

Matthew describes Joseph as "a righteous man." His was a moral uprightness that made Joseph unwilling to expose his pregnant fiancee to public shame and humiliation, but which also made Joseph unwilling to marry her, and so he "planned to dismiss her quietly." God had other plans, and in a dream God informed Joseph of those plans.

The question for Joseph then becomes a question of conventional wisdom and common decency versus radical faith and obedience to the living God. Where shall he invest his trust? In God's promise and command, or in currently accepted practice that passes for righteousness?

Put that way, the question is not only applicable in our day, but urgent. Whom shall we trust? It is not only our enemies who would cause us to abandon obedience and lose faith. Sometimes it is our friends and neighbors and the prevailing morality of society that tempt us to buy into attitudes and adopt behaviors that are inconsistent with the faith.

Such attitudes as, "Helping the poor is a matter of charity, not of justice. And therefore, it is purely voluntary, a good holiday time activity. After all, many of the poor choose to live that way."

Such attitudes as, "The problem in Africa in general and the Horn of Africa in particular is not lack of food but overpopulation. Starvation may be cruel and hard to watch, but as Ebeneezer Scrooge once observed at this very time of year, it does decrease the surplus population."

24

And what of this matter of choice that has in the past few decades become enshrined as the idol before whom all Americans are expected to bow down and do obeisance? The culture genuflects reverently before the altar of Choice. Political leaders preach secular sermons about preserving the Freedom to Choose. But where are the voices that speak of the morality of that which is chosen? Is there no longer a distinction between good and evil? Do we really believe that all choices are equally good? If we do not, then how do we develop the ability to do what Isaiah describes: "Refuse the evil and choose the good"? And how do we teach that skill to our children? How do we help them develop moral gyroscopes that spin in a direction consistent with the gospel?

If the freedom to make choices is worth defending, then the morality of the choices people actually make is worth debating.

If our neighbors would have us believe otherwise, would have us deny that there are morally inferior and morally superior choices, then we are in a situation not dissimilar to that of Joseph: guided by the urbane worldly wisdom of conventional morality.

So when you hear the great blaring, banal voice of the culture beckon to you with all the subtlety of a gum-cracking streetwalker, think of the child, the one named Emmanuel which means God is with us — with us in our struggle to live by faith and by values consistent with that faith, not by the values of convenience and amoral choice.

If *that* were all there were to this text — Dayenu! It would have been enough.

But there is one last item, and that is the baby himself, the child who is *our* Emmanuel, *our* guarantor of God's promises, *our* sign that God is with *us*.

Jesus is our Emmanuel; not merely a *sign* of God, but the *Son* of God, incarnate, embodied deep in the flesh of Mary's child.

The sign God gave to Ahab entailed little risk on God's part. The signs God gave to Noah, to Abraham, and to Moses — rainbows and stars in heaven and sticks turned to serpents — entailed little or no risk to God. But God's own Son, entrusted to the frail and feeble hands of humankind — what greater risk could there be than that?

This is our assurance that God is not asking us to do anything that God is not willing to do: to take a risk. In our case, the risk is trusting God and keeping the faith, despite all invitations to do otherwise.

His name shall be called Emmanuel — which means, "God is with us." To trust that it is so is a risk worth taking, a Spirit-empowered choice worth making. Not only can you believe it; you can bet your life on it. Dayenu! It *is* enough.

Christmas Eve/Day
Luke 2:1-20 (C, L)
Luke 2:1-14 (RC)

For All The People

Year after year, we are drawn to this night: This night with its carols, its candlelight, its communion, and the combined fragrance of pine, poinsettia and perfume. (Is that Passion or Poison you're wearing? Or maybe it's Polo!) The gentle poetry of Luke's story draws us, too.

Why is it that we are so drawn to this night, I wonder? There are, I suppose, as many answers as there are people in this room.

Some are here because they are believers, faithful followers of the Christ. You are here to celebrate the nativity of your Lord. In the name of the Christ you worship and adore, I bid you welcome.

Some are here because they once believed and would like to believe again. You come with the "remembrance of love and peace and shared hopes over many years now gathered into one great longing,"[1] a longing to be with God, to become whole; a longing that the emptiness you now know too well might at last be filled. In the name of the Christ you long for, I bid *you* welcome.

Some are here because, although they neither believe nor hope to believe, still they respect the tradition or honor the wishes of family members and friends. You come because you would not, by your absence, spoil the Christmas of those you love. In the name of the Christ, the God of your fathers and mothers, I bid *you* welcome.

"For behold, I bring you good news of a great joy for *all the people.*"

To all of us — believers, unbelievers, and those who cannot be sure from moment to moment whether or not they believe — to all of us is born in the city of David a savior, who is Christ, the Lord.

His birth is good news of a great joy for *all the people* precisely because it is God's gentle and loving way of overcoming the distinction between believers, doubters and unbelievers.

The announcement of his birth is made not to Caesar Augustus nor Quirenius. Not to Herod or Annas or Caiaphas. Not, in other words, to the head honchos and grand high pooh-bahs of the political and religious establishments. The heavenly heralds of the Christ Child's birth seek out instead mere shepherds — blue-collar guys who pulled the graveyard shift, doing an unglamorous job in the wee hours of the workaday world.

There is no angelic debate over the shepherds' worthiness to be the recipients of so great an announcement. No differentiating between believing, doubting and unbelieving shepherds. Luke gives us no indication that God selected these particular shepherds because of their superior moral or spiritual credentials. Nor did the angels segregate the pious shepherds from those who went to temple only on Passover and Yom Kippur. No such distinctions are made. Just the flat-out announcement of good news of great joy for *all the people.*

How the world needs to hear this unifying message this Christmas! This Christmas when ethnic and religious differences account for the torture, rape and murder of thousands in and around Bosnia.

This Christmas when anarchy reigns in Rwanda and warring parties care little about the resulting starvation of literally millions of human beings.

This Christmas when religious intolerance and racial bigotry make themselves felt and heard in such sundry forms as neo-Nazism in Germany, cross-burning Klansmen in America, and in a Southwest Virginia county, a silly fight turned ugly over whether to call a two-week school recess a Christmas break or a winter break.

This Christmas when Christian denominations are fixated with making and multiplying distinctions: conservative and fundamentalist churches on the basis of biblical interpretation and certain moral issues; moderate and liturgical churches on the basis of racial and gender-based quotas and their own favorite moral and political agendas.

This Christmas when families know the sundering stress of job loss, the destructive dynamics of anger and distancing, the divisive potential of competing demands for limited time and resources.

This Christmas when many in our midst know an echoing emptiness in their lives, an estrangement from friends, a loneliness due to loss — loss of a life or loss of a love — and wonder why God allows this to happen and ponder how they can possibly go on.

This year, when people are not at one with themselves, their families, their friends, their neighbors, their employers, their church or even their God, we **need** good news of a great joy for *all the people*.

More than that, we need the very One whose birth the angels announced. Precisely this One: for like all babies, he is the fruit of the union of his mother and his father. And unlike any other before or after him, this one unifies in his own being both divinity and humanity. In him, God and mortals are at last at one: at one with each other and at one with themselves. That is why his birth is and can be good news of great joy *for all the people*. For he alone is God incarnate among us, sharing our fate and our lot, our struggle and our sense of alienation from self and others.

True man, he knows our frailties and failings, our sinful tendency to make and multiply distinctions between people and make them the basis for division.

True God, he takes these frailties and failings into his own divine being and essence and overcomes them. Not by overwhelming us with celestial power and might, but by joining us in those two universal human realities that unify all mortal beings, birth and death, whose symbols in our faith are manger and cross.

All of us were born and all of us will die. The birth of this holy child transfers those universal realities from the chaotic and divisive realm of fear and terror to the unifying realm of hope and expectation. His birth and death make relative all other distinctions and pointless all divisions based on those distinctions. For if God and mortals are at one in him, then what other distinction — racial, religious or political — can divide us, from God or from one another?

This savior is born to *all the people*. He is born not to demand our faith, but to engender it and enable it. The incarnation of God's holy love for all people, he invites our faith and makes that faith possible.

"For behold, I bring you good news of a great joy for *all the people*." To you — to all of you: believers, disbelievers and unbelievers alike — to *you* is born this day a savior, who is Christ, the Lord.

In the name of this unifying savior, I bid you welcome. Oh, come let us — let all the people — adore him, the savior, who is Christ, the Lord.

---

1. John Vannorsdall, *Dimly Burning Wicks*, Fortress Press, Philadelphia, 1982, p. 23.

Holy Love And Herod's Love

You must understand something about Herod the Great before you can understand what caused him to kill all the baby boys in Bethlehem and the surrounding area.

In the thousand years that lay between King David in Old Testament times and King Herod, no king of Israel wanted to be loved by his people more than Herod the Great. It was a consuming passion for him.

He played the political game with consummate skill. Although a member of the royal family by birth, Herod ruled at the pleasure of the Roman emperor, and his story includes intrigues with Anthony and Cleopatra and friendship with Octavius who later was called Caesar Augustus. Herod's task was to balance the needs and demands of Rome with the hopes and desires of his own people. The truth is that that was an impossible task. The vast majority of Jews in first century Palestine had no use whatsoever for any king, Jewish or otherwise, who collaborated with the despised Roman invaders. Herod himself was anathema to them.

But still, he tried. To his credit, he established something Israel had lacked since the days of King Solomon — a harbor at a seaport city he built and called Caesarea. He built a royal palace, a theatre, and an ampitheatre and a good many fortresses in outlying areas. But the greatest tribute to his desire to win the love of his people was the rebuilding of the Temple at Jerusalem.

Though Herod himself was indifferent to his Jewish faith and heritage, he saw this as an opportunity to win his people over. The priests threw up incredible roadblocks. They complained that only priests and Levites could be allowed to build the temple and — alas — none was skilled at construction. So Herod undertook an intensive training program and taught them how to build.

The priests said the Temple precincts are places for prayer and study of the Torah — God's sacred word. And so they decreed that the sound of hammers might not be heard in the Temple precincts while the building was going on. So Herod arranged to have the stone quarried and shaped miles away and then moved quietly into place!

Herod wanted the Temple to be more grand than Solomon's Temple, so that he might be thought of as a king more grand, more benevolent, than Solomon himself. Even the rabbis went on record as saying, in the words of one contemporary Jewish historian, "One who has not seen Herod's temple has not seen a beautiful building." Maybe, just maybe, Herod thought, the people will see me as their promised messiah.

This is the background you need to understand the story of Herod's brutal murder of the holy innocents, the baby boys of Bethlehem. Herod's story, at one level, is the story of a frustrated desire to be loved.

Herod wanted the love of his people and he would tolerate no competition, stop at nothing to eliminate his rivals. Wise men from the East came seeking the newborn "King of the Jews." Their arrival, precipitated by a celestial sign of an auspicious birth, alerted Herod to the advent of a challenger. And so Herod's fit of jealous rage. And so the slaughter of the holy innocents.

Why does the church recall and remember this brutal and terrifying story on the Sunday after Christmas? Part of the answer is that it has to do with the birth of Jesus and therefore comes close to the Nativity. Another part of the answer is that, hearing this story, we are reminded vividly that Christ was born to die a violent death. We remember that we cannot separate birth from death or Christmas from Good Friday, Bethlehem from Calvary.

I would suggest a related reason: We have in the Christmas story and in the Herod story a study in contrasts in styles of loving.

There are some striking similarities, to be sure. Herod is a king who wants his people to love him. Throughout the Old Testament, God is acclaimed as Israel's king. And he, too, wants his people to love him.

Herod is jealous of his people's affection. "Jealous" is a word also used to describe God: "Behold, I, the Lord your God, am a jealous God"; a God who will not tolerate any rivals, any competitors for his people's allegiance and affection.

But there the similarities end, and the styles change radically.

From all accounts, Herod does not so much love his people as he is consumed by a passionate need to *be loved by them*.

God, on the other hand, first loves his people, and seeks thereby to prime our pumps to return his love.

Herod's passion is centered on himself and his own desires and needs. God's passion is centered on his beloved and on our eternal welfare.

To put it as succinctly as possible: Herod's love is a love that is willing *to kill* for the beloved.

God's love is a love that is willing *to die* for the beloved.

And greater love hath no one than this: not that he kill, but that he lay down his life for another.

At Christmastime, we are never far from the love of God. We experience it in things soft and tender; in memories sweet and fragrant; in stories poignant and touching.

This morning, the First Sunday after Christmas, we bump up against the sacrificial side of God's love, and the high cost of that love.

God's Son — Mary and Joseph's baby boy — is spared death at Herod's hand. But only for a few decades. The baby Jesus will grow and preach and heal and teach. Befriending outcasts and sinners, he will reveal, embody, enflesh, make real the love of his Father God. And he will lay down his life that we — his beloved — might live.

What, then, does this mean for us? I suggest a few things:

- In all the circumstances of our lives, we remember with

33

what sort of love God loves us. Not with Herod's love: selfish, punishing; but with holy love: giving, freeing.

- We remember that we have been bought with a price — that having been so loved and so set free, we are now able to pass that love on, knowing that our needs are met and cared for by a loving God, sometimes precisely in our giving and our selfless loving of others.
- We remember the holy innocents slain at the hands of a jealous tyrant, no matter how that remembrance intrudes upon our lovely Christmas celebration.

Wise men were led to Jesus by following a star, and their safe return was assured because they followed a dream. Jesus was delivered because Joseph followed a dream and took refuge in Egypt. The Holy Family returned safely to Israel because Joseph again heeded not one dream, but two!

Children and families need dreamers today, no less. And more than dreamers, people who act to bring into reality the visions God graciously grants them. People who envision and go out of their way to ensure the physical, emotional and familial safety of God's little ones. For many, that vision necessarily includes children conceived but not yet born. For others, the focus is on the already-born.

Each of us and all of us collectively need to attend to the vision and act in a manner consistent with the vision God grants us. Sitting by idly while children perish is not a godly option.

The birth of the Christ child, together with his inevitable violent death and glorious resurrection, has the power to free us from the deadly deception that is Herod's love, and free us for the living truth that is holy love.

Those who have been apprehended by the vision never say, "It's only a dream"!

Christmas 2
John 1: (1-9) 10-18 (C)
John 1:1-18 (L, RC)

Light In Darkness, Speech From Silence

This season, the boundaries of darkness are pushed back. A light shines in the darkness and the darkness is powerless to extinguish it.

Darkness has always been a potent metaphor for those things in life that oppress and enthrall us, frighten and intimidate us, cause us worry and anxiety and leech the joy from our lives.

We know darkness in our *physical* lives when illness is close at hand, when we lack the basic necessities of life — food, shelter and clothing.

We know darkness in our *emotional* lives when we are burdened with worry, confusion, fear, grief, guilt or hopelessness; when we live with violence or addiction or both.

We know darkness in our *social* lives when relationships fail, when the blessing of solitude gives way to the burden of loneliness, when we cannot make meaningful connections with other human beings.

We know darkness in our *political* lives when we cannot organize our communities and our society in ways that are just and equitable to all, when nations ruin their economies in the name of protecting themselves from one another.

We know darkness in our *spiritual* lives when the chasm that separates us from God remains unbridged from either side, when we know an estrangement from God, from other human beings, and from ourselves; when prayer seems an empty exercise and worship a performance offered to an absent audience.

Darkness symbolizes the evils with which we are entirely too familiar.

Some years ago, two of my children and I went caving. We were part of a group that explored a cave in Giles County, at the foot of Mountain Lake, where the movie *Dirty Dancing* was filmed.

Three rooms and several hundred yards into the cave, the leaders had the group stop, sit down, be as quiet as we could be, and turn off our headlamps. One by one the lights clicked out until we were enveloped by an utter and impenetrable blackness. It was the most profound darkness I have ever experienced. It made no difference whatsoever whether your eyes were open or closed; it was all the same, and you literally could not see your hand in front of your face.

After a while, the leader turned on his headlamp, and what a difference one little six-volt flashlight made! It cast enough light to push back the darkness and enable us to see one another, the room we were in, and the pathway out.

While the lights were still out, the leader had asked us how hard we thought it would be to find our way out of the cave without any light. We all said it would be impossible, and any attempt would be not only futile but also dangerous, since we could not see the hazards, the slippery places, or tell the difference between a five-foot and a fifty-foot drop.

The leader agreed and then said, "This particular cave is pretty popular. People come here at least every week, and sometimes several times a week. Were you to get stuck in this cave without a light, your best bet would be to wait for someone else to enter the cave and find you."

It takes no great imagination to make the connection between the darkness of that cave and the darkness we know in our lives; between the light from our leader's headlamp and the light of Christ, the Light of the world. We wait for One who enters our darkness, finds us and brings us out.

This season the boundaries of darkness are pushed back. A light shines in Bethlehem's darkness and the darkness is powerless to extinguish it.

But let's not jump to premature and unwarranted conclusions. A baby is weak and vulnerable, fragile and open to attack. Right from the start, as we heard Luke tell the story, the Christ Child is exposed to harm: his mother Mary's labor induced by a grueling 80-mile journey; a stable for a birth room; a manger for a bed — harsh hay and straw the only mattress for his delicate, newborn skin. And, according to Matthew, Herod in a murderous rage waiting to snuff out this life right here, right now.

John's witness is true: The light indeed shines in the darkness. But it is not yet a blinding light. It is a gentle glow, a thing of grace and tender beauty. It is the first light of the Christ Child, God's own Son, sent to find us, lost in the night with no light to find our way, and hazards all about us.

Ancient tradition called Jesus the Dayspring — the first ray of light of God's new-dawning day.

Other lights must first be kindled before our rescue is complete: the candlelight of that last supper on Maundy Thursday; the soldiers' torchlight of Good Friday; the dull hellfires of Holy Saturday; the glorious brightness of the empty tomb on Easter morn; the Spirit's flame at Pentecost; and the world-redeeming radiance of Christ's promised return.

What we celebrate this 12-day season is a birth, and as such, a beginning. This season the boundaries of darkness are pushed back. A light shines in the darkness and the darkness is powerless to extinguish it.

For this season, that is enough. A birth. A beginning. A ray of hope — but more than that, an assurance that while we still know dark corners and fearsome shadows in our lives, God is with us. Our rescuer has found us and will remain with us until our deliverance is complete.

He dwells not in unapproachable light, but couches his radiant glory in the thoroughly approachable flesh and blood of the Virgin's child.

That same flesh and blood he gives graciously to us under the forms of bread and wine.

It is his gift of love to us this Christmas. Today we see his light shining in the darkness.

Today we hear his word, the word made flesh, piercing the silence.

Today the boundaries of darkness are pushed back. A light shines in the darkness. A light shines from Bethlehem's stable. A light shines in our hearts. And the darkness is powerless to extinguish it.

**Epiphany Of The Lord
Matthew 2:1-12**

Light From And For The East

Dear Robert,

It was good to spend some time with you over Christmas break. I really enjoyed hearing about your semester in India, and am so glad you had that opportunity. We sometimes tend to pull our worlds in around us like a down comforter on a cold night. There is nothing like living in another country, immersing yourself in another culture, to expand your horizons.

I have begun to work on a sermon for Epiphany. As I do, my mind keeps returning to your observations and questions about other world religions and the bold, universal claims of the Christian faith. I want to think "out loud" (or should we say *on paper*?) about some of those issues, thus feeding two birds with one crumb: continuing our delightful conversation, and clarifying my own thinking on the matter, in light — especially — of the Epiphany story.

You said that Paul's description of the people of ancient Athens, "I see how extremely religious you are in every way," might well be said of the people of modern India, too. You saw that virtually nothing in their entire culture or way of life is without reference to or roots in their religious beliefs and practices. Hinduism, Buddhism, Islam, Sikhism and other major world religions have profoundly formed the heart and soul of the Indian people. As with Christianity, however, not all the consequences are positive. The movie *Ghandi* vividly portrayed the historical tensions and even bloodshed between competing religions and sects, especially Hindus and Muslims.

I was particularly fascinated by your encounter with the street vendor. You were puzzled by the inclusion of the likeness of Jesus on an obviously Hindu painting, and by the merchant's easy incorporation of Jesus into the pantheon of gods. You said he seemed genuinely pleased to acknowledge and acclaim Jesus as yet one more deity. We who are familiar only with the monotheistic religions of Judaism, Christianity and Islam find such polytheism shocking and confusing, almost like a kind of spiritual promiscuity. Meanwhile, they sometimes see our insistence on *one* God as spiritually impoverished and remarkably lacking in religious imagination. That's just one indicator of the religious and theological gulf that divides us.

You are quite right when you say that we have much to learn from these neighbors. We may not appreciate their reverence for literal "sacred cows"; our sensitivities concerning race and class may be offended by the lingering remnants of the caste system; but you and others have detected among them a sense of the mystery and sacredness of life that is for the most part unavailable to modern Westerners. And how many among us can lay claim to as disciplined and intentional a spiritual life as typifies the life of many you met during your semester there?

Time was when we dismissed these people as benighted heathens, "lesser breeds without the law (or gospel!)," and adopted a haughty, patronizing attitude toward them. But as I read Matthew's story of the Epiphany — indeed, all the lessons appointed for Epiphany Day — I wonder: How is it that we ever came to adopt such a sad and arrogant posture?

Please do not misunderstand. I am not saying that one religion is as good as another. I am not endorsing the sappy sentiment that "it doesn't matter what you believe, so long as you are sincere." And I am certainly not commending that gauzy, vapid and condescending attitude we Americans are so fond of: tolerance. What I am suggesting is that God did not despise the religion of the Magi, eastern astrologers not numbered among the covenant people of God, and neither may we.

Indeed, it was precisely the devotion and discipline of the Magi that led them ultimately to the Christ child!

Matthew's way of telling the story suggests a complementarity between Christianity and the world religions. The Magi, without any apparent recourse to the Hebrew scriptures but relying only on the traditions of antiquity and the tenets of their own religion, follow a star in the belief that it will lead them to the birthplace of an important ruler. They follow that star all the way from their homeland — possibly Persia, modern-day Iran — to Jerusalem. That is, their native faith and instinct bring them a long way in the right direction. But then they must do that thing that males — ancient as well as modern, I think — hate the most: They must stop to ask directions! "Where is the child who has been born king of the Jews?" Herod summons the chief priests and scribes and they provide the answer: Bethlehem.

"Hunger for God is a common human trait and deserves respect wherever it is found,"[1] someone has written. The Magi exemplify such hunger. That hunger impels them to travel a long way. Their religion points them in the right direction. But neither their hunger nor their religion is capable of bringing them all the way to God incarnate in the Babe of Bethlehem. Short of the goal, they need detailed information; something more specific than the meandering of a star in the sky. Those who are knowledgeable about the Bible are consulted, and are able to provide the needed directions. And the Magi, thus informed, are able to complete their journey, worship the Christ child and offer to him their gifts.

Is any of this making sense? What I am suggesting is that other religions not only prepare people, they actually lead people God-ward. But people need something more if their wanderings are to culminate as did the journey of the Magi. They need specific direction. The scriptures and those knowledgeable about them are best positioned to provide that direction.

It is crucially important to note that such direction is not toward a principle, a precept or a proposition. As with the Magi, it is direction toward a particular *person*: Jesus.

I recall a conversation with an elder statesman of the church a few years back. He had been part of a group that had engaged in high level theological discussions with Buddhist scholars. After two full days of conversation, the Buddhists said to their Christian counterparts, "We appreciate all that you have shared with us about your faith. But you have not said very much about the one thing that fascinates us most, and that is Jesus. Please, in the time that remains, tell us more about Jesus." This churchman was as dumbfounded as he was embarrassed! His group had intentionally focused on those things they thought Christians held in common with Buddhists, thinking to concentrate on Jesus in a subsequent meeting. Those of another faith reminded them that the single most riveting feature of Christianity is Christ!

We who have been reared in the faith — and in a culture that thinks it is familiar with Jesus — sometimes lose sight of the fact that Jesus truly is an intriguing, captivating and fascinating character. That should be no surprise, for he is God's unique bringer of salvation for all humankind. Though such Christian claims may be offensive to some, it is the offense of particularity, the gospel's scandalous message that God wills the salvation of *all people* through the crucifixion and resurrection of this *one man*, the One the Magi journeyed to adore.

We serve no one well when we say that each religion generates its own valid way of salvation. Nor do we serve the truth when we teach that our particular brand of Christianity is the final and decisive form of faith in Jesus. It is Jesus Christ who is the unique incarnation of God's Truth. Our task is to bear witness to that Truth. By becoming ever more knowledgeable about the Bible, we become better equipped to direct people toward that Truth. But knowledge alone is never enough. We need to go a step farther than did the highly knowledgeable scribes and chief priests in the Epiphany story. They gave accurate directions, but did not themselves accompany the Magi to their destination.

What a different story this would be if they had! Picture it: Jews and Zoroastrians kneeling beside each other, worshipping together and offering their considerable gifts to the newborn king. It was not so then and — sadly — it is not so now. Ironically, that is one of the very reasons the Child was born and will die and rise again — to reconcile the considerable differences between people: racial, ethnic, social, economic, political and religious. The Magi came to worship the King; Herod hatched a plan to assassinate him. That set of facts alone cautions us against absolutist claims about our religion versus their religion. For it is not finally our or any religion that saves us. It is precisely and irreplaceably the one who is Lord of all: Jesus!

All for now. Blessed Epiphany to you and yours.

In his love,
Mark

---

1. Winn, Albert C. and Joseph A. Burgess, *Proclamation 2 Commentary — Epiphany*, Fortress Press, Philadelphia, 1980, p. 12.

**Epiphany 1
(Baptism Of The Lord)
Matthew 3:13-17**

A Long Obedience In The Same Direction

We live in a microwave world. A hurry-up, get-to-the-point, move-it, move-it, move-it, world!

We want what we want and we want it **now**! We want freezer-to-table meals in 15 minutes at the outside; we want 0 to 60 acceleration in 8.5 seconds; we want the phone answered in 3 rings or we're hanging up; we want that personal pan pizza in 5 minutes or we're outta here.

No one reads classical literature any more. Why bother when you've got Barnes and Noble, Monarch Notes and Klassic Komix? Or, if you really must, there's always the Evelyn Wood Speed Reading Course. (I'm reminded of Woody Allen's comment about that course. The comedian said, "I took the Evelyn Wood Speed Reading Course. I read *War and Peace* in an hour and a half. It's about Russia.")

The accelerated pace of life has spawned new attitudes and new behaviors. I'll mention only three.

(1) Child psychologists now talk and write about "The Hurried Child": the accelerated offspring who is prodded by well-meaning, well-intending parents to hurry up, grow up, move on to the next stage of development and excel all the while (and anything less than the 90th percentile is an embarrassment).

45

The consequence: children are robbed of one of God's most precious gifts — the unique and irreplaceable gift of their own childhood.

The message the child receives: "What I am is no good. They'll love me when I make them proud."

(2) The idea of a life-long commitment has become almost unfathomable. The "now" — the present moment — is all that counts, and instant gratification is the name of the game.

Two months from now is the distant future, so how can anyone seriously promise, "till death us do part" or "forsaking all others, keep me only unto thee"?

(3) This quote from the book *Time Wars* by Jeremy Rifkin:

> *Many people have so accommodated themselves to the new sped-up time frame of the computer that they have become impatient with the slower durations they must contend with in the everyday clock culture. In clinical case studies, psychologists have observed that computer compulsives are much more intolerant of behavior that is ambiguous, digressive or tangential. In their interaction with spouses, family and acquaintances, they are often terse, preferring simple yes-no responses. They are impatient with individuals who are reflective or meditative.*

(Try preaching to a roomful of them!)

Now not all of the consequences of living in the microwave society are bad.

Rescue squads and trauma teams know the value of a few precious moments. They respond to emergencies with speed, efficiency and an impressive array of life-saving technology.

The microchip has made the laborious processing and retrieval of information quick and efficient. Once-lengthy calculations are now completed in a fraction of a second.

46

A few months ago I had occasion to telephone the United States Embassy in Bangkok, Thailand, to check on the status of a refugee family we've been trying to reunite with a family here for 2 1/2 years.

The call from Roanoke to communications satellite to Bangkok was completed within five seconds of the time I dialed the last number, and no operator assistance was required. (Those with three-year-olds in the house who like to play with the phone when mommy and daddy aren't looking are in no way cheered by this last piece of information.)

It's a microwave world. Perhaps as the baby-boom generation hits mid-life and slows down a bit, so will our society. But I doubt that the pace of life is likely to return to the comparatively leisurely rhythms of life only a few generations ago.

The question for Christians, then, becomes: Given the pace and direction of modern life, how are we to lead our lives as followers of the crucified and risen Lord, Jesus Christ?

There are, as you might well imagine, a number of answers to that question.

One group of Christians answers the question by withdrawing from what they view as the evils of modernity. They cling to an older and simpler style of life and shun the way of the world. While we may admire their discipline and their commitment, most of us do not embrace this vision as the only one for twentieth century Christians.

Other Christians take the exact opposite approach. They uncritically embrace the values and ways of the world. To them, it is God and the church who must adapt to this brave new world humankind has created, if God and the church have any intention of remaining relevant.

This group sees religion as something like insurance or Social Security: a good thing to have, but nothing to go overboard about.

While we may admire the openness, tolerance and adaptability of this group, few of us are ready to be so uncritically accepting of what many of us see as at least highly debatable developments in medical technology, sexual ethics, biogenetic engineering, and foreign and domestic policy, to name but a few arenas.

47

There is yet a third way to be a Christian in the microwave world — a way suggested by the title of a book by Eugene H. Petersen. It is titled *A Long Obedience In The Same Direction — Discipleship In An Instant Society.*

The title is from a quote by German philosopher Friedrich Nietzsche, and is worth reflecting on: a long obedience in the same direction. What shape might a long obedience in the same direction take?

For one United Methodist pastor in Roanoke, Virginia, it took the shape of a 2200-mile hike on the Appalachian Trail, from its beginning in rural Georgia to its terminus in northern Maine. Pastor Ken Patrick began his hike — a spiritual pilgrimage, really — one April, immediately after Easter Day. He concluded the journey in late September. Once en route, he was struck by lightning. By August he was so severely physically wasted from malnutrition that he was hospitalized and returned home for a few weeks of rest and recuperation. With strength renewed, he returned to the point at which he was forced off the trail, and concluded his trek.

The journey was undertaken in the spirit of Saint Francis of Assisi and was appropriately designated "a hike for the homeless." Some folks sponsored Pastor Patrick so many cents or dollars per mile. The proceeds helped open a new day facility for Roanoke's homeless — a place of hospitality and refuge for those who daily hike the asphalt trail.

That's one shape that a long obedience in the same direction has taken for one Christian.

For us as disciples of the Lord Jesus Christ, our calling and our power to lead lives marked by a long obedience in the same direction comes in our baptism. For it is by water and the Spirit that God drowns the old Adam and the old Eve in each of us and makes of us new beings in Christ.

No one said it better than Paul who wrote in his letter to the Romans, "When we were baptized in Christ Jesus, we were baptized into his death. We were buried therefore with him by baptism into death, so that as Christ was raised from the dead by the glory of the Father, we too might live a new life. For if we have been united with him in a death like his, we shall certainly be united with him in a resurrection like his."

Today, the Christian Church celebrates the Baptism of our Lord, that occasion, according to the Gospels, when God announced Jesus' divine identity to his Son and entrusted to him his eternal mission: to lay down his life for the sins of a wayward world.

Remember that immediately following his baptism, Jesus was led by the Spirit into the wilderness to be tempted by the Evil One. Immediately, in other words, Jesus was tempted to abandon his long obedience in the same direction. He resisted that diabolical temptation, and in his preaching, teaching, healing, reconciling, restoring, liberating ministry, Jesus continued that long obedience in the same direction. On the cross of Calvary, he pursued it to its inevitable end.

This Jesus God raised from the dead. His long and perfect obedience in the same direction is the salvation of us all, through no merit of our own.

Indeed, in spite of our miserable record, in spite of the fact that our lives are littered with broken commitments, abandoned resolutions and half-hearted devotion, God is ever faithful. Jesus, God's Son, is the fulfillment of God's word through Isaiah the prophet:

> *Behold my servant, whom I uphold,*
> *my chosen, in whom my soul delights;...*
> *He will faithfully bring forth justice.*
> *He will not fail or be discouraged*
> *Till he has established justice in the earth;...*

By working in us the miracle of faith, by making of us new beings in Christ, Jesus is indeed establishing justice and righteousness in the earth.

For what is just and what is right in God's eyes is a long obedience in the same direction, and a long obedience in the same direction is precisely the sort of life the risen Christ empowers us to lead. The baptismal font or baptistery is the debarkation point for this spiritual pilgrimage.

Our world is and likely will remain a microwave world, instant, impatient, petulant, confusing.

A long baptismal obedience in the same direction is God's gift to us, enabling us to face the inconstancy, the instability, the inconsistency, and the vacillation of such a world while maintaining our identity, our commitment, and our sense of purpose, meaning, value and worth. Jesus' long obedience is not just a wandering, a meandering, in any old direction, but a purposeful march in the direction of Golgotha and the empty tomb, in the direction of faithfulness, steadfastness, loyalty, integrity, commitment and suffering love finally vindicated and validated by eternal victory!

Think of your life as a piece of music. Life in the microwave world provides you the staccato notes, the quick and sometimes dissonant voice. By itself, it is confusing and lacking in substance or form. It may even seem chaotic and annoying.

A long baptismal obedience in the same direction provides the sustenuto, the sustained voice, the continuo line. It gives body and substance to the piece. By itself, it could become tedious or dull.

But when the sustained voice undergirds and supports the staccato notes — when life in the microwave world is sustained and supported by God's gift of a long baptismal obedience in the same direction — then life is a magnificent fugue — beautiful, rich, multi-textured, varied; surprising yet graceful and grace-filled.

Such a life is beautiful music; played and sung to the glory of the composer God: Father, Son and Holy Spirit, into whose eternal name we are baptized!

Spirit-anointed Son Of God The Father

"Glory be to the Father, and to the Son, and to the Holy Spirit."

"I baptize you in the name of the Father, and of the Son, and of the Holy Spirit."

"The grace of our Lord Jesus Christ, the love of God and the communion of the Holy Spirit be with you all."

"I declare to you the entire forgiveness of all your sins, in the name of the Father and of the Son and of the Holy Spirit."

"Praise him above ye heavenly host. Praise Father, Son and Holy Ghost."

In more ways than we might at first imagine, our liturgy and hymnody is saturated with references to the Trinity — the fundamental, bedrock Christian teaching that the God believers worship and adore is one God in three Persons: the God whose name is "Father, Son and Holy Spirit."

Our reading today from the Fourth Gospel is an excellent example of just how deeply this trinitarian theology is embedded in the witness and teaching of John the Evangelist. John the Baptist sees Jesus, calls him the "Lamb of God," says that this younger man existed before him, and testifies that God has revealed Jesus as the Son of God who baptizes with the Holy Spirit, a revelation attested by the descent of the Spirit upon the Son.

51

Few would cite this as a major trinitarian text. The Great Commission with its dominical command, "Make disciples ... baptizing them *in the name of the Father and of the Son and of the Holy Spirit*" is more obvious, as are the overtly trinitarian greetings and salutations of Paul's epistles. The power of *this* passage, along with many others in John's Gospel, lies in the subtlety of its testimony. A homely example by way of comparison: In Veal Marsala, the Marsala wine permeates and flavors the meat. The wine is not itself the main ingredient; but without the wine, the dish is something other than Veal Marsala. Similarly, a trinitarian understanding of the Christian faith permeates John's Gospel. Without the Trinity, his writing is something other than the gospel.

Martin Luther looked upon John, among all the biblical writers, as the preeminent witness to the Trinity. In this, he was in perfect accord with the early church fathers. And in his Large Catechism, Luther emphasized the Trinity as that which "divides and distinguishes us Christians from all other people on earth."

How strange it is, given the sustained biblical and confessional witness to the Trinity, that voices in the church today — sometimes loud and well-placed voices — speak out against the trinitarian name of Father, Son and Holy Spirit. More than a few are suggesting that that name be replaced by the threefold title "Creator-Redeemer-Sustainer" or used interchangeably with other triadic formulas, such as "Mother-Lover-Friend" or "Parent-Child-Spirit."

In part, the intent of these advocates is laudable. They seek to repudiate the unbiblical notion that the transcendent God is male. They denounce the physical, emotional, economic and spiritual degradation of women, especially when such degradation cloaks itself in a mantle of religious righteousness. They decry any attempt to use God as a prop to buttress the wall that holds women back from full and essential partnership in the world and in the church. In these endeavors, they deserve the full cooperation and prayerful support of all believers.

But when they implicate the Trinity and indict the name of the Triune God in these high crimes and misdemeanors, then Christian love and a passion for the Truth requires that we say, "You have gone too far."

For it is not only our liturgy and hymnody that is thoroughly trinitarian; it is not only John's Gospel and the writings of Luther and others; it is God's self-revelation to the church "of every time and every place!" The One Jesus called "Abba, *Father*" reveals the love of God for all people through the *Son* and their *Spirit* enables us to believe. We, in turn, pray to the *Father* through the *Son* in the living *Spirit* of their love.

The sheer and utter givenness of the Trinity — not as a doctrine we fully comprehend but as a mystery before which we bow — is an inescapable part of the web of Christian faith. It is not one doctrine among others, but part of the very fabric of faith, the identity of the God who rescued Israel from Egypt, raised Jesus from the dead and pours out the liberating, vivifying Spirit on the church.

This rubs late twentieth century Americans the wrong way. We like choices. What sort of choice do we have with regard to the triune identity of God the Father, Son and Holy Spirit?

None, whatsoever. ***And that is precisely our salvation***!

Listen: The Trinity is a mystery that is prior to us, and eternally so: the mystery of the God who is before us, yet with us and ahead of us. The God who is Beginning and Finish and History.

We did not think up this God. This God thought us up!

We did not create this God in our image. This God created us in the image of God!

We did not choose this God. This God chose us!

We did not name this God. This God named the Divine Self and us, and now bids us preach, teach and baptize in the name of the Father and of the Son and of the Holy Spirit.

We did not die for this God. This God died for us: the second Person of the Holy Trinity laid down his life, as John predicted in calling him "Lamb of God," and this is nothing other than the suffering and death of the Spirit-anointed Son of God. The same Father in heaven, for Jesus' sake, anoints us with the same Spirit, and we are free.

We are free from our need to search for or imagine or invent or come up with a God who is congenial to our particular interests; who advances our pre-existing agenda.

The sheer and utter givenness of the Trinity simply is our salvation. For when, like John, we encounter Jesus, the Spirit-baptized Son of God and Lamb of God, we encounter then and there the God who created us precisely in order to die for us, the Spirit of whose suffering love kindles in us the flame of faith and hope and love.

Blessed be God: Father, Son and Holy Spirit, now and forever. Amen!

Epiphany 3
Ordinary Time 3
Matthew 4:12-23

Followership

In today's Gospel text, Jesus calls for repentance, expects Peter and Andrew to drop their nets and follow him, and calls James and John to leave their Father Zebedee in the boat without so much as a "So long, see you later."

My task today is to issue that same call to repentance, that same call to radical obedience and decisive discipleship. For that call is urgent and cries out to be issued in all of its majesty and might.

But as preacher of the gospel — the **good** news of God in Jesus Christ — I cannot issue that call in such a way as to imply that any of us is capable of responding to it of our own free will and spiritual strength. If we can't even keep New Year's resolutions any more than 21 days into the new year, isn't it a little presumptuous to believe that we can turn our lives around in such fundamental ways as repentance, renunciation, true obedience and discipleship?

There is a poem that I believe can help us as we grapple with the call to repentance and discipleship. It deals with the very text we have before us today. Listen:

They cast their nets in Galilee, just off the hills of brown;
Such happy simple fisherfolk, before the Lord came down,
Before the Lord came down.

Contented, peaceful fishermen, before they ever knew
The peace of God that filled their hearts
Brimful, and broke them too, brimful and broke them too.

Young John, who trimmed the flapping sail,
Homeless in Patmos died. Peter, who hauled the teeming net,
Head down was crucified, head down was crucified.

The peace of God is no peace, but strife closed in the sod.
Yet, let us pray for but one thing:
The marvelous peace of God, the marvelous peace of God.[1]

Martin Bell, author of *The Way of the Wolf*, has written: "Human beings do not intentionally seek out upside down crosses. Upside down crosses happen. Suddenly. Often without warning. If we can avoid being there, we do. If we can't, we don't. It's really almost as simple as that."

Just so, according to the poem, Simon Peter, Andrew, James and John were "simple fisherfolk *before* the Lord came down; contented, peaceful fishermen *before* they ever knew the peace of God that filled their hearts brimful and broke them too." The strange peace of God penetrates and permeates our every fiber even as dye permeates a piece of unbleached fabric.

The primacy and priority of that peace of God which lays claim on us and lays hold of us: that is what we need to apprehend as we reflect on our own daily need and struggle to repent, renounce, obey and follow.

In today's Gospel text, Jesus says, "Repent" — and he means it!

He goes on to say "for the kingdom of heaven has come near." The rest of Matthew's Gospel can be read as the unfolding of that promise of the nearness of God's sovereign rule. It is Matthew's way of saying, "In Jesus, God's reign draws near to us. In him

56

Isaiah's prophecy is fulfilled: We who walked in spiritual darkness now see the great light of the Lord's Christ. He kindles in us the flame of faith and by the light of that flame we walk and do not stumble."

For in preaching, teaching, healing and exorcising; in being baptized, tempted, tried and crucified, Jesus brings God's kingdom near to people. In Jesus, the time *is* fulfilled, and in him the kingdom of God truly *has* come near. The good news of God's presence, of the nearness, the at-handness, of his kingly rule gives birth to faith and trust. Such faith and trust empowers us to turn from anxiety to peace, from sorrow to joy, from despair to hope, from hatred to love. In a word, we repent. The power and the call so to do come from Christ, who works in us the miracle of faith and repentance.

The second half of the Matthew passage gives us a snapshot of what the God-empowered life of repentance, obedience and discipleship begins to look like. The word Matthew uses three times to describe it is the word "follow."

Jesus said to Peter and Andrew "follow me" and immediately they left their nets and followed.

Similarly, he called James and John and immediately they left their father in the boat and they followed him.

Our culture is not real big on followership. We rear our children to be leaders. "Don't follow the pack," we say. "Get out in front and be a leader." That's not wrong. When our children are entrusted with a task that requires coordinating the efforts of several people — or several hundred people — we want them to feel competent and confident. We want to have done **our** job of equipping them.

But none of us is a leader all of the time. We are more like that centurion in one of the Gospels. You remember, the one who said, "I am a man set under authority" (that is, I have leaders whom I follow) "and I have subordinates" (troops who follow me). That's the way it is in real life, isn't it? Sometimes we lead and sometimes we follow, and most of the time we do both things simultaneously — taking orders from some and giving orders to others.

Why is it, then, that we are so averse to teaching and learning the skills of good followership? In large part I think because it means giving up control. And most of us have a dreadful fear — a deathly fear — of relinquishing control of any segment of our lives.

Indeed, we do not give up control willingly; and God will not take control from us by force or false promise.

So what's the answer? How does God make disciples — followers — of the likes of us?

The only power I know that enables people to loosen their white-knuckled grip on the control lever of their lives is the liberating power of love.

For it is only in a relationship of love — and the trust that is love's constant companion — that we find the freedom to surrender ourselves to another, make ourselves vulnerable to another, trusting that the other will not exploit our vulnerability for selfish purposes. The other reciprocates our love and trust and similarly surrenders control. When, because of human brokenness, either party violates that trust, then forgiveness is the dynamic force that has the power to make the relationship whole again.

That is how God in Christ makes followers of the likes of you and me: by first making himself vulnerable to us; by forgiving us when we exploit that vulnerability, nailing it to a cross; by then loving us into a new life and a new relationship with him and with one another; and finally, by entrusting to us a task of extraordinary importance.

In faith, we trust that Christ is leading us to a place worth going. And trust him we must, for the way is fraught with dangers and the power is not in ourselves to sustain our commitment over such a journey. That power belongs to the one who is our leader and whose followers we are. And when he infuses us with that power, that is when we know the same strange peace of God of which the poet spoke. It is that peace that continually looses our death grip on our lives and frees us to find our lives in giving them up.

As followers, we are a pilgrim people — never quite at our goal but always on the way, sustained by the love of Christ, strengthened

58

by that exceedingly strange peace of God which is no peace, but strife closed in the sod. Yet let us pray for just one thing: the marvelous peace of God.

---

1. William A. Percy. Public Domain.

How Blest Are Those Who Know Their Need Of God

You may be familiar with the story. It is as wonderful as it is true.

A successful businessman was invited, about 15 years ago, to give a commencement address to a group of 61 sixth graders. The youngsters were about to graduate from an elementary school in a very poor part of one of our major cities.

If these boys and girls followed in the footsteps of the school's other alumni/ae, only about six or seven of them would graduate from high school and it would be remarkable if any went on to college.

The business executive began to gather his thoughts in order to compose the customary commencement address. You've heard it: the one that goes, "Work hard, keep your nose clean and your shoulder to the wheel and — with a little bit of luck — you can make it just as I did."

But the speech had a false ring to it. Empty words, the man thought; hollow words. These kids had little reason to hope and even less reason to try to beat the overwhelming odds stacked against them.

The man knew something radically different was called for if he was to make any impact whatsoever, if his presence in their lives was to be more than a momentary diversion, if the children's future was to take a different shape, a different texture.

And so in place of a commencement address, he made a surprising announcement that graduation day. To each and every one of the 61 girls and boys, he made a promise: I will pay for your college education. Completely.

He announced that he had established a fund and had made an initial deposit of $2,000 for each child. To that amount he would add each year until compounding interest and additional contributions would be sufficient to fund the college education of all 61 children.

Six years later, the students were in twelfth grade. All 61 of them! Not one had dropped out. Three had moved away, but they remained in touch with their benefactor, and the promise continued to hold for them as well.

Their grades were far superior to those of their predecessors. In fact, one of the ironies of the situation was that some of the students qualified for and were awarded academic scholarships!

Many of them accepted their benefactor's invitation to drop in on him from time to time. Among other things, they discussed their choice of colleges and careers. An astounding 58 of them finally attended college.

I have heard only periodic updates since that time, and all indicate the same: the lives of these individuals are markedly better than what they would otherwise have been.

Do you see what happened in the lives of these young people? Because the shape of their *future* was changed, thereby also was their *present*. In place of a conditional future ("If you work hard and apply yourself, then you might overcome the odds against you and succeed"), now there was an unconditional promise ("Because the cost of your higher education is paid for — as a gift and not as an acheivement or entitlement — your studies are not in vain. Your efforts have meaning and purpose, and will bear fruit").

In theological terms, it is what we call the difference between law and gospel, between demand and promise. And the business executive's act of benevolence is an excellent and living parable of the gospel.

The sovereign God could say to us, "If you work hard, keep your nose clean and your shoulder to the wheel, then you might overcome the overwhelming odds against you and gain citizenship in my kingdom."

But our Gracious Benefactor chooses another way, and instead makes an astounding promise: "Because I love you, I will assume the impossibly steep cost of securing your final future, and I give that future to you freely, as a gift, now."

Such a magnanimous and magnificent gift — free and unearned — engenders the free response of faith, love, trust and gratitude.

And when that promise becomes part of us, an integral part of our identity, a working assumption underlying and undergirding our every act; when the promised future is something we can count on and eagerly await, knowing that its advent is utterly independent of our success or failure, then the very way we look at and think about and plan for and live our lives is fundamentally altered, and we become new beings, now, in this present moment.

We begin to view life from a different perspective. And the Beatitudes are a perfect window through which to view the breathtaking panorama of life. For through them, we see that when we are poor in spirit, when we mourn, when we are meek, when we hunger and thirst for righteousness — when, in short, we haven't a single credit to our spiritual account — then it is we are truly blessed: blessed because we know our futures are not finally dependent upon our spiritual wealth, the absence of anguish, our puny strength or meager righteousness; blessed because God cannot fill cups that are full, only cups that are empty. When we are empty vessels, that is when we are best prepared to receive the future that is God's promised gift to us, and not our moral or spiritual accomplishment.

Like those 61 boys and girls, our way has been paid by a gracious benefactor. Martin Luther said it well in his Small Catechism: "All this God has done out of fatherly and divine goodness and mercy, though I do not deserve it." And of the Second Person of the Trinity, Luther wrote, "He has saved me at great cost from sin, death and the power of the devil, not with silver or gold, but with his holy and precious blood and innocent suffering and death. All this he has done that I might be his own, live under him in his kingdom and serve him in everlasting righteousness, innocence and blessedness ..."

Because God in Christ has made us citizens of his kingdom, transferring us from a final future secured by our accomplishments to a future guaranteed by divine promise, our lives now, in this present moment, take on a new shape, a new texture. In a very real sense, we live life backwards, moving from death to life. God treats us now as the people will be when his kingdom comes in all its glory. Again, the Beatitudes give us the picture.

Because we have obtained and shall obtain mercy, we are even now free to be merciful.

Because we shall see God, our hearts are even now purified by that promise, for purity of heart is to place our trust in God and God's promises rather than in our own striving.

Because we are and shall be called daughters and sons of God, we are now and in this moment God's peacemakers, called to be about the blessed work of reconciliation in our families, congregation, community, nation and world. As children of God, we are called to take after our heavenly Father.

And because in all these things the kingdom of heaven is ours, we are and will be subject to persecution for righteousness' sake. For the world is ill-equipped and decidedly reluctant to hear and heed God's word of meekness and mercy; unready to receive God's gifts of purity of heart and peace.

So it is precisely in our efforts to live by faith that the Spirit of God holds ever before us the future our Father has promised and the Son has purchased. And we, who know our need of God, are blessed and renewed in the promise.

Drop *out*? Surely you jest! Drop *in*, and talk freely with our benefactor about the choices confronting us. For precisely in the struggle and the choosing, we are blessed.

Blessed to bear witness to a jaded and suspicious world: to announce to each and every one that her way, too, has been paid; that his future awaits him as a gift.

Epiphany 5
Ordinary Time 5
Matthew 5:13-20 (C, L)
Matthew 5:13-16 (RC)

Salt And Light

I was on a bit of a tight schedule that day, so on my way from one hospital to another, I stopped off for lunch at a fast food restaurant, whose name I will not mention. After I got my Chicken McNuggets, I went over to do battle with the paper napkin dispenser. [What mean-minded person invented those things, anyway?] While I was engaged in mortal combat with this stainless steel contraption that parts with napkins as willingly as a mother bear parts with her cubs, and with just about the same amount of shredding and clawing, my concentration was broken by a too-loud voice from behind me.

"You're a preacher, aren't you?" asked the voice.

"Does it show that much?" I winced, as I smiled at the kindly-looking woman who made the inquiry, and whom I did not recognize. I wasn't wearing a clerical collar, but the book on my tray may have given her a clue: *The Death of Jesus in the Letters of Paul.* That's different enough from Danielle Steele and Stephen King that the good woman had reason to suspect that only something as odd as ordination would cause one to engage in such lunchtime reading.

"Yes, I am," I said.

"Where do you do your preaching?" she asked.

For a split second, I wanted to say, "From this big limestone pulpit with an oak reading desk mounted on it." But the Holy Spirit grabbed hold of my tongue and made me give the more straightforward and respectful answer: "At Christ Lutheran Church on the corner of Grandin and Brandon."

That answer *always* causes folks to squint and squinny their eyes and furrow their brows for a moment, as they access their mental map of the streets of Roanoke, and *that* expression usually gives way to the exclamation, "Oh, that green stone church across from Patrick Henry High School."

"That's us," I said, as I finally extracted approximately two dozen napkins from the vanquished chrome box. I was about to invite the lady to join us for worship when she blurted out, "When y'all gonna have another one o' them big yard sales in y'all's parkin' lot? I really liked that last one y'all had."

"When was that?" I asked. I've been at this church going on 17 years now, and there has never been a sale on our lot in that time to my recollection. If my conversation partner was recalling a sale prior to that time with such obvious fondness and glee, it must have been one *heck* of a sale.

"Oh, it was a coupla months back," she said.

I tried to suggest that she may have had us confused with another local church, but to no avail. To her, we were the Church of the Remarkable Rummage Sale.

I invited her to come worship with us, anyway. She smiled and thanked me. I went off to my booth — to eat, to read, and to think of some environmentally responsible use for 23 surplus napkins.

My conversation with the kindly woman disturbed me. Not because she so expertly sniffed out a pastor travelling incognito. (Well, okay, that disturbed me mildly.) But because it provided a glimpse, a quick indication, of how some folks view the church: Holy Holder of Mammoth Yard Sales. For others, it might be Organizer of Oyster Roasts, Barbecues, Bull Roasts and Pig Picks. For still others, car washes and bake sales might come to mind.

And if such things are the operative images *of* the church in the minds of those *outside* the church, then we have some considerable amount of work to do if we are faithfully to carry out the mission described in today's Gospel reading. There, Jesus calls his followers, "the salt of the earth," and "the light of the world," and challenges them to season and preserve like salt, to let their light shine to the glory of God.

"Earth" and "world" could hardly be more inclusive terms. It is clear that they refer not to a race or ethnic group, but rather to all those outside the covenant people of God. If the church is the Body of Christ on earth to whom God entrusts the ongoing mission of seasoning and preserving, of enlightening and illumining, then we need something bolder than bake sales, barbecues, bull roasts and rummage sales to bear bright and salty witness to the love of a crucified and risen Christ.

Rather than talk about those bolder ways, I want to share with you some verbal snapshots of what some of those ways actually look like in life.

Jesus says his followers are "the salt of the earth."

Consider: An employee says to a co-worker, "I know we have a lot of work to do on this project, and I can work overtime on it with you. But that particular Wednesday is Ash Wednesday, and I will be at church for about an hour. That's not negotiable: I simply don't miss that service. I'd be glad to have you join me. We can go back to the office afterwards."

Salt.

Jesus says his disciples are "the light of the world."

Consider: A few months back, we received a letter at the church. It was from a young woman whom we had helped with rent money when her husband moved out on her and her children without warning, leaving her with no income and no resources. Her request had come through the Presbyterian Center in Southeast Roanoke, and we used money from the Pastor's Discretionary Fund to help her, cooperating with other local churches to raise the total month's rent.

In her letter, she thanked us for being there for her in her time of need. She has moved to North Carolina, has a job, and is getting on with her life. She is also going to church, something she said she had not done since childhood. Enclosed was a small check, together with a request that we use it to help someone else in circumstances similar to hers. Light, reflecting and multiplying light.

Jesus worries about salt losing its taste.

Consider: A pastor pays a visit to some folks who have worshipped at the church she serves. In the course of the visit, they share with her part of their spiritual journey. It includes an upbringing in which Sunday morning was a weekly exercise in guilt and humiliation. A lot of shoulds and musts and oughts. A lot of finger pointing and the rhetoric of threats and warnings. Both husband and wife stopped going to church, but sought no other church home, having been told that all others were but tools of the devil. When they did begin to worship elsewhere, the word of grace, of God's unconditional love for the sake of the crucified Christ, found fertile fields in their souls. The wife told of the last church they belonged to, just before their move to this new community. "We studied a book in an adult class," she said. "It was called *Jesus Means Freedom*. The title of that book just about summed it up for me. I now know the freedom that comes from the love of God in Christ." Salt: savory, invigorating salt.

Jesus says, "Let your light shine before others."

Consider: In a letter to all his parishes, a Lutheran bishop shares this witness story from the experience of his son's cancer surgery.

"The surgery was held on the last day of the year, and took longer than expected. The doctor, looking in the traditional area for additional evidence of cancer, found none. He decided to look deeper into the abdomen than the procedure called for, and there he found another small tumor, and evidence of its spread to three other lymph nodes, all of which were removed. I shall never forget his response to my question, 'Why did you look there for cancer when it is not part of the normal procedure?'

"The doctor said, 'You will appreciate this, since I know what you do for a living. I was raised by Jesuits, and felt that I wanted to serve God with my life, too. I went to seminary for a year, but after that, I knew that I would have to serve God another way, rather than through the ordained ministry. So, this is what I do. Now, I know that you, and many others, have been praying for Aaron. I can only report that I felt that I was led by God to look into that part of his body.' "

Light, penetrating light set on a lampstand, illumining all in the household.

The Spirit of the living God is active *in* our lives and *through* our lives, to make us salt and light. The Spirit animates the church which is the body of Christ to pursue the mission Jesus entrusted to his disciples: to let their light shine before others, the earth, the world — those within and without the family of faith.

Bake sales, barbecues, bull roasts and rummage sales do little to increase the illumination of that light or the tastiness of that salt. But when a worker makes time for worship; when a woman and her children are kept from homelessness; when someone is led to say and know and feel that "Jesus Means Freedom"; when a surgeon bears a humble witness to the Spirit's inexplicable guidance, the seasoning quality of the salt is preserved, and the light burns brighter.

Epiphany 6
Ordinary Time 6
Matthew 5:21-37 (C)
Matthew 5:20-37 (L)
Matthew 5:17-37 (RC)

"You Have Heard That It Was Said ... But I Say To You"

The pastor finishes reading the Gospel text and the people squirm more than usual. What will he say? What can he say?

The passage he has just read proclaims a chain of hard sayings, some of them impossibly harsh, condemning sin and strengthening the commandments. Anger, insulting speech, adultery, lust and swearing oaths are all roundly condemned. But it is the stark prohibition against divorce that has the people wondering what he will say.

In the text, Jesus clearly says, "No divorce." The pastor must be faithful to the text. At the same time, he wants and needs to be known as a sensitive, compassionate, caring person. He knows there is hardly a family or an individual in his congregation that has not been touched by divorce or its long, long shadow.

For many, the wound is still gaping; the guilt still being carried about; the hurt more suppressed than healed.

The marriages of some other members, he knows, exist in name only, the couples long since having rent asunder what God once joined together until all that remains is a legal contract, two people sharing little more than an address and a phone number, and a relationship that is mutually dissatisfying if not mutually destructive.

Finally, he fears, there may be a few in the congregation self-righteous enough to want to hear divorce and the divorced criticized as always and in all cases wrong (or at least morally irresponsible) and maybe even beyond the redeeming grace of God. These "give 'em hell" types he fears the most and pities the most as being yet a long, long way from the kingdom.

The pastor wants and needs and is called to speak a clear word, a resounding word in support of lifelong trust, commitment and faithfulness on the part of those who choose to marry. He is called to announce God's will that marriages be permanent, riding out the storms of pride and passion. Brides and grooms promise to remain faithfully committed to each other so long as they both shall live, not so long as they both shall love. They do well to remember Dietrich Bonhoeffer's words to his friends on their wedding day: "It is not your love that sustains your marriage," Bonhoeffer wrote, "but your marriage that sustains your love."

Can he say these things without heaping more guilt on the heads of the already guilty, more grief of the hearts of the still grieving, more sorrow on the souls of the already sorrowful? He knows only a few (but there are indeed a few) who have chosen divorce as the apparently easy way out, a convenient end to an inconvenient relationship. The others have already suffered too much, forgotten by those who used to be friends to say nothing of self-recrimination and the anguish they see in the eyes of children who do not — and perhaps cannot ever — understand.

So the pastor has a dilemma. He stands at a point where the biblical witness and the lives of his people intersect. And the tension is enough to rend him asunder.

Part of him wants to run. To find refuge in the second lesson or the psalm and preach on them instead. Or focus exclusively on that paragraph of the Gospel about reconciling with an estranged brother or sister in the faith before offering one's offering at the altar. That would be a piece of cake compared to this.

But he knows himself well enough to know that precisely when he feels inclined to run, that's the time to stand firm and tough it out. Jacob and his family were blessed because Jacob wrestled with an angel, not with a piece of cake.

Nor can the pastor water down the text, explaining it away with a bit of scholarly misdirection or sleight-of-hand — pointing out, perhaps, that a mere 14 chapters later in Matthew's Gospel, Jesus opens the door to divorce on the grounds of unchastity. No: the stakes are far too high for such theological manipulations. It was precisely such legalism and searching for loopholes and attempts at self-legitimization that Jesus is challenging in this sermon of his. His antitheses ("You have heard that it was said... but I say to you...") set up a contrast between the old way of thinking and living and the new way Jesus teaches about and ushers in.

The religious leaders of the day debated endlessly about what the law *permitted and allowed*; Jesus proclaimed what God *commands*. The people wondered about their rights under the law; Jesus announces God's holy will: the creator's righteous intent that marriages be indissolvable.

So the pastor must allow the prohibition against divorce to stand, and to stand in all its stark and intimidating simplicity. God intends the marriage of one man and one woman to be an unconditional commitment of lifelong faithfulness, come what may. And that is precisely what brides and grooms promise to each other in their vows: "I take you for better or worse; for richer or poorer; in sickness and in health, to love and to cherish, until in death we part. This is my promise to you."

God intends the "come what may" unconditional nature of marriage to be an earthly intimation of God's "come what may" unconditional love for his people.

But as long as those people, scorched by divorce or not, hear with old ears and think only what is legal and permissible, they will miss this point entirely. Worse, they will say to themselves, "As if my life weren't messed up enough, now I've got Jesus against me, too."

The pastor knows his people will not be set free by moralism and demands, by threats and recriminations. That's the old way of hearing and living and believing. They need to hear and appropriate Jesus' new way which is not to relax God's commands and figure out ways around them, but to hear in them God's loving will as good news for their lives, however bruised and broken and burned those lives may be.

And that can happen only when they die to the old, legalistic, Pharisaic way of listening and are born anew to listen and hear as children of God.

The word that kills is precisely Jesus' word: "Moses gave you this law and these loopholes for your hardness of heart."

That is not a concession, but a judgment upon all of you, divorced or not. It is evidence of your stubbornness and your coldness. It is an accusing finger pointed continually at you. You are people with a heart of stone, interested not in hearing and hearkening to God's will, but in manipulating, conniving, and finagling your way around it. You are cold and unmoved and hard of heart and those words describe not a living being, but a petrified fossil, long dead.

That is the word that kills. But that is not the last nor the only word. Jesus speaks another, and that word makes us alive.

He speaks to us this time not as moral guide or judge but as the heavenly bridegroom. As he calls each of us by name and rouses us from our sleep of death, we hear what he is saying to us: "I take you for better or worse; for richer or poorer; in sickness and in health, to love and cherish. You are mine, come what may. And as I have death behind me, not even death or all its fearsome force can part us. Because I live, you shall live also. This is my promise to you."

The one who justly accuses us of hardness of heart is the very one who touches those hearts and speaks to our hearts to revive them and to make them new, soft and warm and open and beating and tender. He speaks forgiveness and reconciliation to the divorced and offers them a new beginning. He cradles in his loving arms those whose marriages are but a hollow shell or a battleground and offers them new hope. He touches the hearts of the self-righteous "give 'em hell" types and invites them, too, into his father's kingdom.

Against such a one, we need no more defend ourselves. From his will, we need no more protect ourselves. For in him and in him alone, our death is turned to life. In his will, and in his will alone, our brokenness is at last made whole.

The pastor finishes reading the Gospel text and the people squirm more than usual. What will he say? What can he say?

He stands at a point where the biblical witness and the lives of his people intersect. And at last, by the grace of God, he sees clearly that that intersection is in the shape of a cross.

Jesus' Countercultural Sermon

Sometimes age and experience force us to reevaluate long held beliefs about the world and the way life works. As idealistic youths in Sunday school and Luther League, for instance, my friends and I vexed and perplexed our ultra-orthodox pastor by arguing against the doctrine of original sin. We were convinced that people were innately and instinctively good. And then we grew up and were "mugged by reality": stung by the selfishness that lies hard by the heart of each and every mortal being, including ourselves.

Some among us once believed in some form of elemental fairness and justice in this life. And then we saw virtuous people suffer great hardship and heartache, while others who lived only for themselves prospered and flourished.

Part of growing up is shedding ideas and notions that fit us no better than toddlers' clothes would fit us now. "Older and wiser" is the phrase that comes to mind.

But sometimes, age and experience reinforce long held views. I have, for example, long believed that the Christian faith is by definition countercultural. What I mean is this: Many of the central tenets and themes of the Christian faith run counter to the prevailing beliefs and values of the society in which we live. A few examples:

Ours is a culture that values material abundance and prosperity; Jesus says, "Blessed are the poor."

Our culture denies death and avoids suffering; the Christian faith unromantically confronts death, teaches that suffering holds redemptive power, and sees the suffering and death of one man as the gate to life for all people.

Our culture makes heroes of rugged *individualists*; baptism gathers God's family into *community*. Indeed, the God we worship — one God in three persons — St. Augustine described as a "community of love."

Our culture warns against mixing religion and politics; the God of the Bible is highly political, and nowhere is the political manifesto of that God more clearly articulated than in the Sermon on the Mount, a portion of which forms today's Gospel reading.

The themes of that sermon are highly countercultural. They ran counter to the beliefs and practices of first century Israel and Rome, and they run counter to the beliefs and practices of late twentieth century America.

From an itinerant rabbi whom faith acclaims as God's only Son comes an astonishing reversal of human values and mortal ways of going about the business of life.

But one glance at the morning news is all it takes to see that the great reversals Jesus proclaims are not very widely in evidence among those who name the name of Jesus:

Serbs and Croats — many of them Christians — murder each other in a protracted and bloody war whose root causes few of us comprehend, and even fewer of us care about.

In our land, where Christians still comprise a plurality if not a majority, there is a growing resentment not only of anti-poverty programs, the effectiveness of which is certainly open to reasonable debate, but more dangerously, a resentment of poor people themselves.

And giving to organizations and efforts to fight hunger — in this congregation and many communities of faith — is dramatically down, despite increased need and — for many who could respond — increased income.

It is well known that Mohandas Gandhi was a great admirer of the Sermon on the Mount. A confused reporter once asked him, "If you like the Sermon on the Mount, then what do you think about Christianity?" Gandhi replied, "I think it would be wonderful." Gandhi's reply is at once both comical and a stinging indictment of Jesus' followers.

Our Lord's sermon describes an old way (an eye for an eye, for example, and a tooth for a tooth) and then commends a new and better way (turn the other cheek; do not resist an evildoer.) Such countercultural preaching typifies the mission and ministry of our Lord. Recall some other of his statements:

"The first shall be last and the last first." That's countercultural!

"Whoever would be great among you must be your servant. And whoever would be first among you must be slave of all." That's countercultural!

"Those who would save their lives will lose them, and those who lose their lives for my sake and the gospel's sake will save them." That's countercultural!

"Those who exalt themselves will be humbled, and those who humble themselves will be exalted." That's countercultural!

God's way of being with us runs counter to our expectations of who God is and how God ought to act. God comes as a baby, cradled in a feed trough; God dies on a cross, convicted like a common criminal. The countercultural mystery of the gospel is that that coming and that cross are more powerful than any regime, any power or principality in the world; more powerful than any sloth, apathy or lovelessness in our hearts and souls, for that coming and that cross simply *are* the power of God's perfect love.

When we hear the stark and startling demand Jesus makes in the closing verse of today's text, "Be perfect," we do well to remember that it is precisely God's perfect love and not our moral and spiritual striving that has the power to perfect us. God's perfect love emboldens and sustains us to swim against the currents of our culture when those currents flow counter to the perfect will of the holy and righteous God.

When we hear the demand of perfection and shudder at the impossibility of fulfilling it, we do well to remember that the

God who says "Be perfect" is the same God who said "Let there be light" ... and there *was* light! This God brings about his holy and perfect will by calling into being that which did not previously exist: light in darkness, order out of chaos, countercultural followers of Jesus from those whose lives were once indistinguishable from those of the surrounding culture.

People who hear Jesus' sermon and hearken to it find themselves living countercultural lives, by the grace of God. For when people learn to turn cheeks, surrender cloaks, go second miles and love their enemies, they demonstrate that they are living by the values of God's coming kingdom rather than by the values of the present age.

Those who place their trust in the God whose perfect will Jesus' sermon proclaims find themselves no longer consumed by the love of power, but perfected by the power of love. And in late twentieth century America, my friends, that sort of lifestyle is *definitely* countercultural.

Epiphany 8
Ordinary Time 8
Matthew 6:24-34

Don't Sweat The Numbers

Once upon a time in a land not far from here, there lived a nation of people. By and large, they were good people, decent people, industrious and hardworking people. They lived commendable and often praiseworthy lives, dedicating themselves to such endeavors as caring for home and family, building better communities and schools, and helping one another in a variety of ways.

These were people you and I would be delighted to have as neighbors. They had only one quirk, one idiosyncrasy: They were obsessed with numbers. Absolutely consumed by them.

Numbers, numbers, everywhere you looked, there were numbers! Every year was known by its number. Every day was broken down into numbered parts and people wore jewelry to tell them what number it was: 2:45 in the morning or 7:15 in the evening. Busy people were quick to remind you: "There are only 24 hours in the day, you know."

Every house had a number. Every car had metal tags with numbers on them. Major roads were known by numbers like "Route 419" or "Interstate 81."

The government even sold little medallions with numbers on them for people to hang around the necks of their pet dogs, and this was not optional but mandatory. A dog without a number?

Why, that was an illegal dog! A K-9 in violation of some city ordinance with a long number and several sub-numbers.

These people were so infatuated with numbers that when babies were born, the proud parents would send out cards that would say, "We've got a new baby! She was born at 3:25 a.m. on 10-12-95, weighing in at seven pounds, six ounces and she's 21 and a half inches long."

But, since those numbers were subject to change, a more permanent number was needed. And so the parents would fill out a form, send it in to the government Agency in Charge of Numbers, and that agency would assign the child a nine-digit number that would be hers for life. Somebody else might have the same name, but, by golly, nobody else would have the same number!

As the child grew, she would be identified by still more numbers. People would say such things as, "She's in the 95 percentile height, 75 percentile weight. Her IQ is 114 and her GPA is 3.22. She can run the hundred in 12.3 seconds and she's got a part-time job. Where? At 7-11; makes 4.65 an hour.

And, most people agreed, that last category represented the most important category of numbers: the numbers that people earned, inherited or accumulated.

When, for instance, a person worked for a company, then every week or so, the company would take some of its numbers and transfer them to the employee. The bigger the number transferred, the more people tended to respect the job and, hence, the person who held the job: "He only makes 12,000 a year; she makes 53,000 a year!"

People with bigger numbers got to live in bigger houses, drive fancier cars and generally enjoy what folks called "the finer things in life."

There were basically three things that people could do with their numbers: they could spend them, save them, or give them away.

The spending was easy and fun. The people were so hardworking and industrious that there were lots of things they would sell you in exchange for some of your numbers. Spending numbers was so much fun, in fact, that most people spent more numbers than they actually had! They did this by promising to pay bigger numbers in the long run in exchange for the privilege of obtaining an item or service now and paying smaller numbers for many, many months to come.

Saving numbers was a different matter. It was something most people agreed was a good idea, but found it hard to do. I mean, when you've already promised away 25% of your future numbers for the next 360 months for a house, and another 10% for 60 months for a car, after the government has already taken 28% to run the country and keep its promises, and that agency that assigns nine-digit numbers to newborns has taken 7.65%, well, that doesn't leave very many numbers to feed, clothe, educate and entertain the family. Consequently, this nation's savings rate was about the lowest in the developed world.

It was in the area of giving numbers away, however, that the people exhibited the most unusual attitudes and behavior. They were among the most generous people in the world. When they saw a need (such as hungry people or victims of a disaster or a new program to help unfortunate children) many of them were quick to take some of their numbers and share them with the needy. And this sharing made them feel good and happy. So although their savings rate was among the lowest, their giving-away rate was about the highest in the world.

Now the strange thing about the situation was this: if someone would tell these people, "You know, you really ought to try to save more of your numbers," they'd smile and shuffle their feet and say, 'Yeah, you're right. But it's darn hard, you know.'"

But if someone were to suggest that they ought to consider giving some of their numbers away to this need or that cause — maybe more numbers than they gave away last year — then some of the folks got downright angry and offended.

Strange, isn't it? Tell them they ought to do something they're not doing and they smile and agree with you. Suggest they ought to do more of something they already do and enjoy doing, and they get offended. Well, there are some cultures that are difficult to understand.

Be all that as it may, what concerns us this morning is the fact that numbers became so important to these people that their obsession spilled over into the religious realm.

I don't mean a mere preoccupation with the number of members on the church roll or the size of the number that the church had managed to accumulate in the bank or even the fact that they had a collection of sacred scriptures one portion of which was called, "The Book of Numbers." No, I'm talking about their actual understanding of God.

They preferred to call God by the mathematical term "The Infinite." They believed God was the ultimate source and giver of all numbers, and so if you pleased The Infinite and were among The Infinite's chosen people, then The Infinite would bless you with bigger numbers. Conversely, if you had little numbers, or no numbers at all, then clearly you were not among The Infinite's favorite and beloved people. Clearly, The Infinite was displeased with you.

People longed to be one with The Infinite. Bigger numbers were closer to infinity, they reasoned, so it followed that the way to become one with The Infinite was to acquire the biggest number you could. And all the people set themselves to this task — religiously! All those, that is, except the ones with little numbers or no numbers at all. They figured that they were so far from The Infinite that there was no point in even trying.

Into this busy and industrious and compulsive situation came the Stranger. He was as mysterious as the square root of a negative number. Something there was about him that was as inexpressible as the quotient of a number divided by zero. And to the people he bore an unsettling message. His message was this: "Don't sweat the numbers. Numbers are not where it's at. The Infinite cares for you infinitely, no matter what your number!"

Some of the people, especially those with little numbers, were intrigued by the Stranger and his message. Quickly, he developed quite a following.

He spoke to the people of The Infinite's love and benevolence. He told them their needs were cared for because it was the nature of The Infinite to give and give and give and still be undiminished.

84

And, he added, it's the same way for you and me. The way to the truly happy life is to be relatively unconcerned about the numbers. "When you give," he said, "that's when you get. You're like a candle lighting other candles. No matter how many times your light is borrowed and divided and shared, it is never diminished. Indeed, the more it is shared, the brighter the world becomes.

"Just so, The Infinite gives to you more abundantly than you can give away."

And then he added, "You can never obtain The Infinite. The Infinite is by definition the highest number imaginable *plus one*. And it's that 'plus one' that always puts The Infinite out of reach."

Someone asked him, "Then how do we become one with The Infinite?"

He replied, "You can't." The people were stunned, shocked, silent. But the silence was redoubled when he continued, "The Infinite has become one with you!"

"That's absurd," challenged the Chief Number Cruncher of the Temple. "The Infinite cannot become finite."

"The Infinite" replied the Stranger, "can become anything or anyone The Infinite chooses to become."

"And," the Chief Number Cruncher said with a sneer, "I suppose you would have us believe that The Infinite has chosen to become **you**."

"Your words, not mine," said the Stranger.

"Blasphemy!" said the Number Crunchers.

"Heresy!" cried the Mathematicians.

"Cancel him, negate him!" cried the people. "And let his nine-digit number be eradicated."

With many such shouts, they put the Stranger to death.

But then The Infinite did what The Infinite does: he gave. He gave new and never-ending life to the Stranger. And then the people knew that the Stranger had been right all along. His new life was The Infinite's way of saying, "Q.E.D.: Quod Erat Demonstrandum." The Stranger proved that which was to be proved:

He gave so much that he died without a number to his name. Yet he was one with The Infinite. Indeed, he **was** The Infinite!

People saw that their obsession with numbers was self-defeating. The Stranger's message was trustworthy and true. Was then. Is now. And so it bears repeating:

When you give, that's when you get. No matter what your number is, The Infinite cares for you infinitely. And so, my friends, don't sweat the numbers.

Transfiguration Of The Lord
Matthew 17:1-9

Main Features And Coming Attractions

You go into the movie theatre, find a seat that's suitable, clamber over some poor innocent slumbering in the aisle seat, taking pains not to step on toes or lose your balance. You find a place for your coat, sit down, and get ready to watch the movie. The house lights dim; the speakers crackle as the dust and scratches on the soundtrack are translated into static, and an image appears on the screen. It is not the film you came to see. It is the preview of coming attractions, a brief glimpse of the highlights of a film opening soon. The moviemakers and theater owners hope the preview will pique your interest enough to make you want to come back and see the whole film.

On the Mount of the Transfiguration, Peter, James and John, the inner circle of Jesus' disciples, were given a preview of coming attractions. And today, on the Festival of the Transfiguration, so, too, are we — a splendid preview of Jesus radiant in divine glory, his mortal nature brilliantly though only momentarily transfigured; a dazzling preview of his divinity, unalloyed and perfectly pure, shining in glory like the very sun. A sneak preview, in other words, of Easter, the triumphant climax of the epic love story between God and humankind.

But like the preview in the movie theater, this is not the film that is showing today. It hasn't opened yet; it can't be seen in its entirety. Only a glimpse to arouse interest and stimulate curiosity. Those whose interest is piqued will have to wait, will have to come back.

Peter, for one, thinks that's a punk deal. This is the big picture he's been waiting to see. He's viewed enough of the melodramatic healings and documentaries featuring Jesus the teacher. Peter's recent confrontation with Jesus over the rabbi's depressing talk about rejection and suffering and dying is still fresh on his mind. His soul still stings from his master's words, "Get behind me, Satan, for you are not on the side of God but of mortals." Peter wants no more of that kind of talk, no more of that kind of picture. He wants action, big, bold, spectacular. This vision on the mountain, with Jesus, Moses and Elijah in celestial conversation, this is more like it. No: not *like* it; this *is it*! This is what he had hoped for ever since he dropped his fisherman's nets and hitched his wagon to the rabbi's rising star.

"Thine is the kingdom and the power and the glory" will soon become "*Mine* is the kingdom and the power and the glory" if only these giants of the faith will let him hang out with them. So naturally he offers to build three booths, three dwellings — it's a way to prolong the moment, to forget the main feature about to be played out and jump ahead to the coming attraction he and the others are here previewing.

Once, in a conversation with a colleague, I observed that this story suggests an appropriate name for some churches. "You know," my friend replied in agreement, "now that you mention it, I don't think I know of any Transfiguration Lutheran Churches."

"I wasn't thinking of Transfiguration Lutheran Church," I said. "What I had in mind was 'Three Booths Lutheran Church.'"

For how often does the church seek not to *seize* the moment, but *freeze* the moment? Typically it is some moment of glory in the congregation's life, some fond memory of a person, a practice, a program.

A clerical acquaintance tells this story: "When I came to my last congregation as Associate Pastor, I collected some bruises as a result of running headlong into a few booths that had been erected along the way. One I remember especially well. It had to do with a particularly cohesive group of young people who had just graduated from high school, thus concluding their involvement in the congregation's youth group. This *was* a special group: they were blessed and they were a blessing. People recalled their energy, their enthusiasm and their commitment with obvious and appropriate fondness. And then some would go on to say, 'There will never be another youth group as good as that one.' Wham! Peter couldn't have built a better booth himself!" We know a moment of glory when we see one, and when we see one, we want to seize one; and when we seize it we want to freeze it.

It's a real no-brainer to figure out the effect that particular booth had on the youth who were left behind, struggling to become a group themselves. That booth may as well have had the shape of a coffin, because it effectively killed youth ministry in that congregation for about a year or so. Nobody *meant* to do that. It's just that our instincts, like those of Peter, make us go for the glory and revel in it and hope it will go on forever, and be disappointed when it passes — as inevitably it must — to make way for God's new thing.

It is a perpetual temptation for the church to become a religious museum, for its leaders to become curators and caretakers, with energies diverted and devoted to the institutionalization of the past, especially moments of glory past. But God has so designed the universe that time marches on. Moments of glory fade. Exciting previews of coming attractions end and the real story we came to see unfolds.

God has done this, I think, not only out of divine necessity, but out of divine mercy and compassion as well. Constant ecstatic stimulation, like constant conflict, can and does lead to emotional burnout. As with Jesus, Peter, James and John on the mountaintop, what goes up must come down. And that's a mercy. A cause for thanksgiving and not lament.

All of which brings us back to those six men on the mountain, and the voice from the cloud. This particular preview of God's coming attraction is in fact related to the main feature that is about to unfold. God's voice from the cloud confirms it. For when that voice declares, "This is my son; **_listen to him_**," Jesus' disciples, then and now, do well to obey. Listen to him. What is he saying? He just got finished talking about how he must be rejected and suffer and die. *That's* what we need to listen to. The glory will come. The Transfiguration is a preview. But first must come the main attraction.

The main attraction: a fitting description, for when Jesus spoke of his crucifixion, he said, "When I am lifted up, *I will draw all people to myself*." That's the main attraction: the cross of Christ, hard though it is to understand, hard though it is for our Lord to bear.

Obedient to the divine command, "Listen to him," we focus on that cross this coming season of Lent, and attend carefully to the story that unfolds. The empty tomb of Easter is for now a coming attraction, and the Transfiguration is the preview. Jesus has literally to go through Hell before that picture opens, and with it, the graves of all God's beloved daughters and sons.

Books In This Cycle A Series

Gospel Set
God In Flesh Made Manifest
Sermons For Advent, Christmas And Epiphany
Mark Radecke

Whispering The Lyrics
Sermons For Lent And Easter
Thomas Long

Christ Our Sure Foundation
Sermons For Pentecost (First Third)
Marc Kolden

Good News For The Hard Of Hearing
Sermons For Pentecost (Middle Third)
Roger G. Talbott

Invitations To The Light
Sermons For Pentecost (Last Third)
Phyllis Faaborg Wolkenhauer

First Lesson Set
Hope Beneath The Surface
Sermons For Advent, Christmas And Epiphany
Paul E. Robinson

Caught In The Acts
Sermons For Lent And Easter
Ed Whetstone

Tenders Of The Sacred Fire
Sermons For Pentecost (First Third)
Robert Cueni

What Do You Say To A Burning Bush?
Sermons For Pentecost (Middle Third)
Steven E. Burt

Veiled Glimpses Of God's Glory
Sermons For Pentecost (Last Third)
Robert S. Crilley

Second Lesson Set
Empowered By The Light
Sermons For Advent, Christmas And Epiphany
Richard A. Hasler

Ambassadors Of Hope
Sermons For Lent And Easter
Sandra Hefter Herrmann